KATHI LIPP

WITH CHERI GREGORY AND
ERIN MACPHERSON

THE

Mom

PROJECT

HARVEST HOUSE PUBLISHERS
EUGENE, OREGON

Unless otherwise indicated, all Scripture quotations are from The Holy Bible, New International Version®, NIV®. Copyright © 1973, 1978, 1984, 2011 by Biblica, Inc.® Used by permission. All rights reserved worldwide.

Cover design by Emily Weigel

Cover photos © Hintau Aliaksei / Shutterstock; OpiaDesigns / Creative Market

Published in association with the literary agency of WordServe Literary Group, Ltd., 10152 South Knoll Circle, Highlands Ranch, CO 80130.

SOCIAL STYLE and The SOCIAL STYLE Model and TRACOM are marks of The TRACOM Group. All content is used with permission of The TRACOM Group. Visit www.socialstyle.com for more information.

THE MOM PROJECT

Previously published as *21 Ways to Connect with Your Kids*
Copyright © 2012 Kathi Lipp
Published by Harvest House Publishers
Eugene, Oregon 97408
www.harvesthousepublishers.com

978-0-7369-7198-0 (pbk.)
978-0-7369-7199-7 (eBook)

The Library of Congress has cataloged the earlier printing as follows:
    Lipp, Kathi, 1967-
    21 ways to connect with your kids / Kathi Lipp with Cheri Gregory.
      p. cm.
    ISBN 978-0-7369-2967-7 (pbk.)
    1. Parent and child—Religious aspects—Christianity. 2. Child rearing—Religious aspects—
      Christianity. I. Gregory, Cheri. II. Title.
    BV4529.L57 2012
    248.8'45—dc23

                         2012006821

Printed in the United States of America

      18 19 20 21 22 23 24 25 26 / BP-SK / 10 9 8 7 6 5 4 3 2 1

To Justen Hunter

Besides making me a mom, you've made me a better person,
a better writer, and a more faithful follower of God.
And I thank him every day for you.

Acknowledgments

Great thanks go to Erin MacPherson, who kept this book going even when I was not. You are so talented, and I am so grateful.

Thanks to Cheri Gregory for sharing your insight into the personalities with all of us who are trying to parent those kids who are just like us, and nothing like us.

Thanks to all the parents who shared their stories. You made this a much better book.

Thanks to Amanda, Jeremy, Justen, and Kimber. I know you will be able to use these stories with your therapist someday.

So many thanks go to my team: Angela, Sherri, Brooke, Mikkee, Jen, Lynette, Christina, and Kimberly. Thanks for keeping this dog and pony show going, and for loving God and loving families, and serving both.

Thanks go to Rachelle Gardner and to LaRae Weikert, Rod Morris, and the rest of the Harvest House team. No one need remind me that God put me in the best hands in publishing.

Thanks to our families—the Richersons, the Lipps, and the Dobsons—for giving us the best stories.

And finally to Roger. Two single parents. Blending a family. Of four teenagers. If surviving that is not proof of what an amazing godly man you are, nothing is. You rock my world.

Contents

Bonus Connections

Part 1

Preparing to Connect

The Book I Almost Didn't Write

I argued with God for a long time before writing this book.

When I originally came up with the idea to write a book about connecting with your kids, I was on a "Mom High." My husband, Roger, and I had been married for five years, and we had successfully blended a family. Two of his, two of mine, my cat, our dog.

Even the challenges I'd had with my stepson, Jeremy, after Roger and I got married were a mere memory. We had learned to care for each other, hang out together, and enjoy each other. And my relationship with my stepdaughter, Amanda, was growing, and we loved being together. All our kids would come over for Sunday night dinner and would often hang out during the week. While I knew we were far from perfect parents, I was excited that Roger and I both had close relationships with our kids.

But then all that happy parenting became a memory.

My son, Justen, was going through a tough time in his life. He grew cold and distant from me. We were fighting and arguing and going through an awful, awful time.

And I needed to write a book about how to be close to your kids.

I cried out to God. I felt betrayed by him. I had poured all this love and energy, time and prayer into my son, and he was barely speaking to me. I felt like a failure. I felt like a fraud. And on the rare occasions that Justen and I had a conversation, I would curl up in a ball and cry as soon as we were done talking. I hated where our relationship was.

I talked with my husband about not writing the book. Not out of shame or embarrassment (and trust me, I felt both of those) but simply because I felt like the principles I had practiced didn't work. My son was distant from me, and all the praying in the world was not helping. I asked friends to pray for Justen, pray for me, and pray for what this book was supposed to be about.

I wrote much of this book during my desert time with Justen. I had nothing to hold on to but God's Word, especially Philippians 4:6— "Do not be anxious about anything, but in every situation, by prayer and petition, with thanksgiving, present your requests to God."

So I waited and I prayed. And I prayed some more.

And now, seven years after I finished writing this book, I have a different, longer perspective. God used time and the healing that only he can bring and restored Justen to a good place. It's taken a lot of time and a lot of prayer. But when I talked with Justen's counselor, the one thing he said that I will never forget is this: "Justen felt safe enough with you to express his anger to you, because even with all of his anger, he never questioned your love for him."

And now, after going through all that, my publisher and I have decided to update this book. My kids are adults, and I'm happy to report that we have a close, loving relationship with each of them (and now one son-in-law, Shaun, whom we adore).

I'm afraid that each of my kids have gone through some pretty hard times. And the bad news? Yours will as well. They are going to go through loss and disappointment and sadness, and they are not always going to behave as if all this "connecting stuff" will make a difference. But let me tell you, seven years after writing this book, I am even more convinced of one thing: It does.

Trust the process and trust your parenting. Be open to change when God or common sense or the needs of your child tell you to. But here is my conviction: We are probably better parents than the world makes us believe. God has given you everything you need. You are not always going to feel like connecting. Do it anyway. Your kids need you to invest in them when they are young so that when they are older, they don't ever have to question your love for them.

Why You're a Better Parent than You Think You Are

can tell you one thing about yourself right off the bat: You're a better parent than you think you are. I know that's a bold statement (especially since we've never met), but if you are anything like me and my friends, someone needed to tell you that.

I remember looking at the other moms at church, the dads out in the parks pushing their kids on the swings, and just *knowing* they all had it way more together than I ever would. Those thoughts started exactly one day after I became a parent.

It was time for us to check out of the hospital with Justen, who at one day and nine pounds and four ounces was just about the most terrifying thing I'd ever seen in my life. I was having a small (OK, enormous) panic attack. I couldn't believe that the authorities, whoever they were, were going to let me take him home. Didn't they realize I'd never handled a human baby before? What kind of broken system do we have that would let me (me!) take home this not-so-tiny baby boy?

And that's when I knew I was sunk. In my mind, no one had ever had those thoughts before. All around me were happy couples who were dying to get their babies home and do what? I really had no idea. But I felt as though everyone else had been given a secret manual, and I had missed that day of orientation.

And the feeling persisted. All the other moms acted as if they had been parenting for decades. They had their parenting methods all picked out and were parenting on purpose.

I had a sneaking suspicion that they had their kids sleeping through the night after three days, were breastfeeding without tears, and woke up hours before their children so the house would be clean and activities laid out—activities that were not only creative but also educational. I felt like the world's biggest loser of a parent.

But then something miraculous happened. I started talking to other parents. I mean *really* talking. And guess what I found out?

I found out they were just as unconfident, strung out, and secretly ashamed as I was. They too thought their kid was the only one to ever have a meltdown in the middle of Whole Foods. They too thought they had the only child on the planet who insisted on wearing his Spiderman underwear on the outside of his pants. They also thought that everyone else cooked homemade spinach muffins for their kids every morning and did alphabet-training drills starting at age two.

If you can relate to any of this, let me give you a few words of encouragement.

God gave the right parent to the right kid. There are days when this statement couldn't feel further from the truth. You feel ill-equipped to meet your child's physical, emotional, and spiritual needs. Because, for the most part, you are. God wants you to rely on him and the people he's surrounded you with. You are not designed to do this parenting thing alone, even if you are a single parent. There are no gold stars for parents who never ask for help.

God gave the right kid to the right parent. All those things that God needs to grow in you to draw you closer to him? He sent those in a neat little package called "your child." Each of my kids has taught me something about myself—often things I would choose to ignore if given the opportunity. I would have never thought that I had a patience problem, for example, until I had a patience tester named Kimberly. But there is no chance to ignore such things when they need to be bathed, fed, and loved pretty regularly. I had to confront the parts of me that needed, desperately, to be more like Jesus—and often, I needed to confront my problems with a lack of patience before Kimber woke up from her twelve-minute nap.

Prayer is key. For years, when a kid issue reared its ugly head, I would go to my friends, I would go to my mom, and I would go to my wall of "how to raise a great kid" books to find the answer. I needed answers, and I needed them quick! But as my friend Erin MacPherson, author of *The Christian Mama's Guide to Having a Baby: Everything You Need to Know to Survive (and Love) Your Pregnancy,* says when it comes to pregnancy as well as parenting, "Go to God before Google."

God will direct your heart as you parent. From day one, what I really needed was to know the heart of God and to let that direct me as a parent. Yes, I'm a big believer in wise counsel, but I am a bigger believer in not using God only when things hit the crisis stage (or the principal's office).

• ● • ● • ● •

Now, if you have a couple of years under your parenting belt, would you do us all a favor and tell the other mothers around you what went wrong?

- Tell us how the helpful junior higher you now are raising once threw a toy and knocked out her older brother's tooth.

- Tell us that you faked dizziness so they wouldn't release you from the hospital and you could stay another night.

- Tell us that your one and only prayer for the first year of your daughter's life was, *Dear God, please don't let me screw her up.*

When I was in high school, I had a youth leader named Emily Nelson. Emily had it all together. She'd married a great husband and started having great kids. Emily was the kind of person that I would spend a lot of time comparing myself to. You know the kind. You think to yourself, *I bet they're the kind of parent that grows their own organic food while teaching their kids French, as opposed to my kid who learned how to read from frequent exposure to packages of Chicken-Dino-Nuggets.*

So imagine my glee when I read this essay by Emily about being a not-so-perfect mom:

> As we cruised down the coast, singing along to Veggie Tales, I tossed carrots to my 3 sons who quickly gobbled them up. We arrived at the beach with our fresh-from-the-library-checked-out book about seashells and started collecting. After making sandcastles and letting them bury me neck deep, I pulled out the ice cream maker and made homemade, organic ice cream. I snapped a funny picture of them. "This one is for the scrapbook!" I exclaimed, and they tackled me with a hug. This was a perfect day, but… it never happened.
>
> My REAL beach day started with screaming them into the car to beat traffic, telling them to forage the van floor if they were hungry, and throwing beach toys onto the sand, while I collapsed in my beach chair devouring the latest *People* magazine. I didn't even bring the camera.
>
> Looking back I'm tortured with what I didn't do with my kids: take them hiking, educate them in museums, have family devotions. And I moan about what I did do: harsh words, wishy-washy discipline, and over-involvement in non-family activities. I look at the creative moms, the outdoorsy moms, the homemade-everything moms, the spiritual moms and think they parented so much better than I. Yet one day, as I was recounting my lack of mothering skills to my 27-year-old, he encircled me in a hug, saying, "Mom, you did just fine!" That boy never has to buy me another gift, as he gave me the gift of peace that maybe, just maybe, I did okay.

Every parent has struggles. Every parent has those nights when they toss a loaf of bread and some peanut butter on the table and call it dinner. But every parent also has those moments—probably more often than not—when they are a rock, an encourager, and a God-given gift to their children.

Your parenting road is going to have its share of take-the-hubcaps-off potholes. And it may be a long time before you hear the words, "Mom/Dad, you did just fine!"

But remember 2 Corinthians 12:9: "But he said to me, 'My grace is sufficient for you, for my power is made perfect in weakness.' Therefore I will boast all the more gladly about my weaknesses, so that Christ's power may rest on me." God is sufficient for all your needs. Even your parenting needs.

You see? You really are a better parent than you think you are.

3

Special Blessings: When You Have a Challenging Situation

As a teen, I was part of an organization called Teen Missions that would send kids all over the world to do building and evangelism projects. Our training ground was the swamps of Florida. Why there? My theory was that the swamps were so bad that wherever you were going on the mission field would seem like a little bit of heaven after your time in Gator Country.

It was a big job, keeping all those kids in line. And when you were having a rough day, and maybe not behaving in the way you should, you were given a "special blessing." These blessings were things like cleaning out an outhouse...and trust me, no one wanted to be so blessed.

As a parent, I've felt as if some of my experiences have been "special blessings"—things that have been given to me to grow me as a child of God and as a parent. Here are some of the "special blessings" I've had as a parent:

- Getting to parent teens (at one time we had four, ages thirteen to eighteen)
- Being a stepparent
- Being a single parent

Each of these situations required extra grace, extra prayer, and extra reliance on God.

We are going to be talking about how to connect with your kids, but each of the above situations can offer some unique challenges. That's why I've included a section near the end of each connection activity to address these.

Teen Challenges. These are tips and ideas to turn each connection into something your teen would want to participate in.

Step It Up. This section is for those step and blended families and the unique challenges those parents face.

Suggestions for Singles. If you are a single parent, this is the section to encourage you and help you along.

A Note to Dads

If you are a dad reading this, you get major bonus points. I congratulate you on your decision to invest in your kids in a real and tangible way.

Most of the dads I've talked to feel a natural connection with their sons. They've already bonded through sports or movies or some other common interest. It's usually the girls that terrify them.

In addition to the connections you'll make in this book, may I suggest another resource for you dads? *88 Great Daddy-Daughter Dates* by Rob and Joanna Teigen is an excellent guide to hanging with and talking to the second most important girl in your life.

Connecting with Your Kid's Personality

I know my kids pretty well. I know that Kimberly could spend all day watching *Gilmore Girls* while Justen would rather play board games so late into the night that I would cross him in the hall as I was getting up and he was going to bed. I know that both of my kids are into steampunk, which, when it comes to literary genres, is about as far as you can get from my women's fiction. I know that Justen has an affinity for numbers (the kid can remember multiple car license numbers), and I know that for some reason both of my kids had a soft spot for our mean, cranky cat, Zorro, whom no one else seems to like.

But I don't know anything about your kids. I don't know what makes them squeal with excitement. What quirks they have. Or what they'd do tonight if they were given twenty dollars, ten gallons of gas, and a chauffeur to drive them anywhere they wanted.

And you're probably wondering how I can help you connect with your kids if I don't know them.

I thought of that too, and I have a plan. Based on the SOCIAL STYLE Model of personality assessments (used with permission of The TRACOM Group), we have provided specific ways to connect with your child's personality. Of course, in order to do that you have to know what type of personality your kid is. So my friend and personality expert, Cheri Gregory, has created a simple questionnaire that will help you to determine your kid's personality type. And then, throughout this book, we'll help you find ways to best connect with that child's unique personality.

So to get started, circle the letter(s) in front of the statement that best describes your child:

Assessing Your Kid's Personality *by Cheri Gregory*

In photos, my child

- E) is always smiling, often with head cocked to one side
- AN) sits up straight and looks serious
- D) has an "Are we done yet?" look that conveys what an imposition the photo shoot is to his/her schedule
- AM) slouches, leans against someone, or lies all the way down

When on the playground during recess, my child

- E) loves playing in a group
- AN) knows, follows, and enforces the rules of the game
- D) plays to win
- AM) often watches from the sidelines

When it's time to clean up or do chores, my child

- E) can turn work into a game or a dance
- AN) likes knowing where everything belongs and putting it all away
- D) thrives on responsibility and chore star charts
- AM) may vanish completely during chore time and magically reappear as soon as the work is all done.

When there's a sudden change of plans, my child

- E) is either devastated (if the change causes disappointment) or elated (if the change causes anticipation)
- AN) is distressed because what should be happening is not happening (and may even accuse you of lying: "But you *said*…")

D) reacts with hostility to the loss of control
AM) patiently rolls with it

Given a choice, my child would prefer to

E) have a party
AN) organize his/her belongings
D) play a competitive game/sport
AM) "chillax"

When relating to authority figures for the first time, my child

E) tries to charm them and make them laugh
AN) analyzes their expectations and strives to meet them
D) challenges them, testing their right to be boss
AM) wants to hang around with them (especially if they're nice)

When it comes to clothing choices, my child prefers

E) bright!
AN) coordinated outfits in subdued hues
D) functionality
AM) comfort

I would describe my child's walk as

E) prancing
AN) pacing
D) striding
AM) moseying along

*Of the following, the one that I've observed
is most important to my child is*

E) playing
AN) organizing
D) doing
AM) resting

My child seems to learn best by

    E) talking

  AN) seeing

    D) listening

  AM) getting hands-on

My child enters a competition and does poorly.
To him/her, the worst part of the entire experience is

    E) disappointing you; not giving you something to cheer about

  AN) making mistakes; trying to figure out what he/she did wrong

    D) not being #1

  AM) the stress of the entire experience

When learning a new skill, the thing that
will upset my child the most is

    E) corrections

  AN) illogical instructions

    D) failure to progress rapidly

  AM) complexity

The worst part about being sick for my child is

    E) being isolated from people

  AN) the germs, messes, and medications

    D) the to-do list that's not getting done

  AM) not feeling well enough to actually enjoy the R & R

I'm often told that my child is too

    E) talkative

  AN) obsessive-compulsive

    D) bossy

  AM) lazy

My child's response to a group assignment at school is

    E) euphoria that he/she will get class credit for socializing

  AN) resignation that he/she will be the one to make sure the finished product is good enough to turn in

    D) determination to make everyone do his/her part

AM) satisfaction that there are plenty of other people in the group
    to carry his/her weight

*Of the following, the one that I've observed
is most distressing to my child is*

    E) rejection

AN) chaos

    D) powerlessness

AM) disharmony

My child is likely to dislike a teacher/authority figure who is

    E) critical

AN) late

    D) incompetent

AM) insensitive

My child's biggest time management issue is

    E) optimism: acting as if everything will magically work out
    (and, if not, who really cares if he/she is a little late?)

AN) perfectionism: he/she gets so caught up in little details that
    projects often remain unfinished

    D) *energy* management: he/she starts too many projects and tries
    to do them all simultaneously

AM) procrastination: he/she puts things off until the last possible
    moment

*An important contribution my child makes to his/her
friendships and to our family is demonstrating how to*

    E) really enjoy life

AN) care about quality

    D) get things done

AM) live at peace

If we were to plan a family trip together, we'd count on my child for _____ (but then…)

- E) spontaneous enthusiasm and tons of excited questions (but then he/she might forget to pack half the necessaries)
- AN) alphabetized checklists for packing (but then he/she might become stressed from double-checking all the pretravel details)
- D) leadership in setting concrete goals for the trip: where to go, what to see, how long to stay (but then he/she might tire us out with a demanding daily agenda)
- AM) a calm and easygoing presence, with a bit of dry humor that breaks any tension (but then he/she might dig in his/her heels right at the worst possible moment)

Now tally up your kid's score by writing down the number of times you circled each letter:

E _____
AN _____
D _____
AM _____

If you answered:

Mostly Es, your kid is an enthusiastic, social, and creative *Expressive* personality

Mostly ANs, your kid is a consistent, practical, and conscientious *Analytical* personality

Mostly Ds, your kid is a confident, competitive, and bold *Driving* personality

Mostly AMs, your kid is a sensitive, loyal, and steady *Amiable* personality

* Note: some kids are a mix of two or more personality types. So if you find yourself answering questions evenly, that's fine. Just make sure to consider both personality types as you work on connecting with them.

So What Now?

Now that I've whetted your appetite for learning about your kid's unique personality, I'm going to help you to use that information to build a stronger relationship with your kid. At the end of each of the 21 connections that follow, I've included a section titled "Connecting with Each Personality." Those sections will include simple ways to adapt that connection activity to fit the unique needs and desires often associated with each personality type. So as you read through this book and start connecting with your kid, remember to tune in to that child's God-given personality and consider what he or she needs as you connect.

This isn't meant to box your kid in. Quite the opposite. This is meant to give your kids the freedom to be who God designed them to be without you having that nagging feeling that, because your kid doesn't respond to discipline in the way you did, or your kiddo couldn't care less that you praised him publicly, something is wrong. God has equipped each of us with a unique personality, and there are no mistakes!

5

A Quick How-To Guide for Part 2:
21 Ways to Connect with Your Kids

The purpose of "21 Ways to Connect with Your Kids" is to spend time intentionally loving on, caring for, and connecting with your children. And since the point is to focus on connecting with your kids, the last thing you need to do is stress about getting it done according to a certain timeline or doing things the way Mrs. Perfect Mom (or seemingly perfect) next door does it. That's why I encourage you to make this yours. Here are my suggestions on how to get started.

1. Read through all of the connections.

This is your chance to get a feel for all twenty-one of the connections. Feel free to use the margins to make notes as you think of ways to tailor-make each connection to work best for your family.

2. Figure out a timeline.

As I said, I want you to make this yours. So spend some time figuring out a timeline that works for you. Here are a few ideas:

- Do one connection a week for twenty-one weeks.
- Do the shorter connections (3, 4, 8, 10, 12, and 20) on

busy weeknights, then plan to do one big connection each weekend until you've done them all.

- Group the connections thematically like this:

  Week 1: Encouragement (connections 3, 4, 8, and 20)

  Week 2: Time (connections 1, 2, 10, 16, 17, and 18)

  Week 3: Service and Missions (connections 5, 6, and 15)

  Week 4: Legacy (connections 9, 13, 19, and 21)

  Week 5: Passion (connections 7, 11, 12, and 14)

- Figure out a timeline that works for you.

Whatever you do, make sure you plan out when you're going to do each connection and write it down.

3. Find two other friends who want to do the connections with you.

It doesn't matter if they're phone friends, Internet buddies, or face-to-face girlfriends you meet with at Starbucks down the street. Location is not important; consistency is. You just want someone to bounce ideas off of, share triumphs with, and listen when you're struggling.

4. Look over the connections and come up with a plan.

I've provided a variety of ideas, but it's up to you to decide how you'll carry out each connection. Get creative; think about your kid's unique personality and come up with how each connection is going to best work for your family.

Write in your calendar in advance what you're going to do for each day. We're parents, and I have yet to meet one who is able to function at a sane level without an agenda and a to-do list. This will help you to stay on track. You'll also need to make some specific plans along the way. Is there a connection that requires you to order supplies? Baking a certain cookie recipe? Get what you need now.

5. Be flexible.

We're talking about kids here, which means there are going to be those days where your kid just needs to go to bed early or needs some extra snuggle time on the couch. It's fine to reschedule a connection if a certain day just isn't working.

Part 2

21 Ways to Connect with Your Kids

Connection
1

Fifteen Dollar
Family Fun Night

Try This

Plan a Family Fun Night for sometime in the next week.

Making the Connection

Is it *really* possible to feed a family of six and have fun, all for fifteen dollars? I dare you to find out!

When my kids were young, we didn't have the financial capacity to blow hundreds of dollars on family adventures. We never had front-row seats to Broadway plays. Or season tickets to the 49ers. Or fancy dinners at those restaurants where you get to cook your meat over a little grill in the middle of the table.

Instead, we would have "Fifteen Dollar Family Night." One family member (sometimes it was a kid, sometimes a parent) was in charge of the planning. The chosen planner would get fifteen dollars to feed and entertain the troops. Our family experienced everything from a bake-at-home pizza and a DVD of *The Princess Bride* to a home-packed picnic at the duck park followed by an afternoon at the local nickel arcade.

And while these adventures aren't as glamorous as front-row tickets to a Taylor Swift concert, they ended up being experiences that we laughed and talked about for years to come.

We found many benefits to setting aside some time for family fun:

- Not only did Family Fun Night give us an opportunity to spend time together, it forced our kids to plan, budget, and take other people's likes and dislikes into consideration.

- We found that giving the kids the chance to plan the event helped them enjoy this time a whole lot more. Our kids really got into it. Sometimes the event was a surprise to the rest of the family. On another occasion, Kimberly made invitations for everyone in the family so they would know what the evening held (as well as appropriate dress code).

- Having a limited budget has a special magical quality. With such limited funds for a night out, there was no resorting to a dinner out for everyone at your favorite family restaurant followed by the latest movie in the theaters.

Make Connecting Fun

Perhaps the best part about Family Fun Night is the unlimited number of variations. It doesn't have to be fifteen dollars. It doesn't have to be elaborate. It doesn't even have to be at night. You plan according to your family's schedule and budget. Remember, the goal is to have a meal and some entertainment. Here are just a few of the things that you and your kids could do:

- *Dollar Date Night.* Have Costco hot dogs and then head to your town's local dollar theater.

- *Carpet Picnic.* Spread out a blanket and have a picnic in your living room while watching borrowed VeggieTales DVDs. Serving something besides soup would be a wise plan on a night like this.

- *Pizza and Pinochle.* Order a pizza (plan ahead and find a coupon) and have a family game night.

- *City Cinema.* Pack some sandwiches and take advantage of a community-sponsored "Movies in the Park."

- *House Movies.* If you have a projector (or can borrow one) hook it up to your laptop and show a DVD on the side of your house while eating dinner on a picnic blanket or on lounge chairs. If you have a pool, you can take it one step further and do a "Dive-in Movie." Grab some flotation devices and watch the movie from the comfort of your pool.

- *Hot Dogs and Hiking.* Find a day-camp spot and roast hot dogs over an open fire after a walk in the woods.

- *Entertainment Anyone?* Purchase an Entertainment book (www.entertainment.com) for super discounts on meals as well as family entertainment. If you have an indecisive child planning the family fun night, this would be a great help in giving them some ideas.

- *Airplane Food.* Have a paper airplane competition. Go to www.10paperairplanes.com and create a variety of planes. They give great, step-by-step instructions that older elementary age kids can follow. Younger kids will need Mom's or Dad's help. For dinner, have little packages of food (cheese and crackers, carrot sticks) as "airplane food."

- *Karaoke Night.* Borrow a karaoke machine or use your Wii, and make it an *American Idol* style night (but with only adoring fans—no harsh criticism). Pair it with a Make Your Own Sushi dinner. For less adventurous kids, their sushi can be made out of cooked chicken, ham, or cheese on top of rice.

- *Happy Hour Concert.* Happy hour isn't just for the after-work crowd anymore. Many restaurants are offering great food deals. We've found a restaurant that offers two-dollar burgers and another that does half-off appetizers—along with free live music.

- *Dig Out the Gift Cards.* Recently, Roger and I went

through all of my purses, his wallet, and the drawers in our
desks and nightstands and collected all the gift cards we'd
received for various occasions. It was a little embarrass-
ing. We had over forty cards that had various amounts of
money sitting on them. Suddenly, we had a lot of opportunities to use those up for dates for just the two of us or
for some extra special family nights. I bet if you looked
around the house, you would find some gift cards just
waiting to be used on your next family night.

- A couple of times we even threw all the gift cards into a bag
  and picked one randomly to plan some family fun around.
  How excited was Roger when we had to figure out what to
  do with the Best Buy gift card?

Make Connecting Work

Planning a great Fifteen Dollar Family Fun Night doesn't require days
of planning, a litany of schedule finagling, or even a two-hour session
finely chopping veggies and chicken for your well-intentioned-but-
more-complicated-than-it-sounded DIY omelet bar.

Keep it simple. And keep the focus on what it's all about: Connecting with your family. Here are just a few ideas to keep finagling to a
minimum and fun to a maximum:

- *Send an e-vite.* To build up excitement for the evening, you
  or your child could send an e-vite (www.evite.com) to
  every member of the family to let them know what the
  plan is.

- *Write it down.* Remind your family that Fifteen Dollar
  Family Night is coming up by writing it in big letters on
  your family calendar or scrawling it in dry-erase marker on
  their bathroom mirror.

- *Spend some time getting ready.* Don't just throw on a pair
  of leggings and your ratty tennies (unless, of course, your
  Family Night involves doing something sporty like playing

Frisbee). Get glammed up for the occasion and show your
family that you're excited to spend time with them.

• *Put away your cell phones.* I know, I know. Going dark in
  the digital world, even for a few hours, feels so...so, well,
  1996. But try to keep your phone in your purse and let
  calls go to voice mail for a few hours so you can really focus
  on your family.

• *Give your kids full power to plan on their day.* Even if your
  kids don't plan the same way you would have, make sure
  you give them the opportunity to plan the fun. Just think
  of this as training for when your kids get married—they
  will be the most creative and thoughtful spouses out there.

Teen Challenges

If you have a teen going through a "Why can't these people just
leave me alone?" phase, here are some ways to make Family Night a little less torturous:

Discuss timing in advance. Tell your teen when the activities are
going to start and when you expect the festivities to end. This helped
my teens a lot knowing that when family night was done, they could
go out with friends or have some time to themselves in their rooms. If
they know there's a start and an end to your time together, it will be
easier for them to relax a little and hang out.

Let your teen plan. I want to reiterate that if your kid has the opportunity to plan the night, they are much more likely to enjoy what you
end up doing. Just saying.

Bring a friend. I thought that if I allowed Kimberly to bring along
a friend on one of our adventures, the two of them would form their
own little alliance and leave the rest of the tribe. Not so. Kimber
participated with family activities even more when she had a friend
along. It may not be appropriate for every family night, but every
once in a while, inviting a friend along will show you a different side
of your teen.

Step It Up

I'm going to say something radical here. Sometimes it's okay not to blend the blended family.

As Roger and I sought wise counsel, the therapist we were dumping all of our step-problems onto told us, "You are forcing the family. Roger—you do things with your kids. Kathi—you do things with yours."

What? Weren't we supposed to all hang out together, forcing these kids to mingle until we made them like each other?

But we were paying the counselor a ton of money; it probably was a good idea to try what he said.

So Justen, Kimberly, and I did some family nights on our own, and sometimes Roger came along. One night my kids and I ate dinner at home, and then we used some movie gift cards to see *The Prize Winner of Defiance, Ohio* (we'd read the book together) in a theater. We used the fifteen dollars to buy a drink to share and some popcorn. Roger and his kids didn't know anything about the movie, and because it was an art-house flick, they had no desire to come with us. We had a grand time and were able to relax and talk on the way home. Our own little family night.

Roger has often done things with just his kids. Movies, dinners out, and even vacations. Our kids did much of their growing up in different families; it seems silly to try to force too much togetherness.

And now? Our kids love to come home for big family meals and look forward to all going on vacation, together.

Yes, it's great to be able to blend everyone together, but remember: each of your kids needs their own parent to themselves without having to share with a step.

Suggestions for Singles

For single parents, try partnering up with another single friend every once in a while to mix things up. Even just watching a movie at someone else's house can be enough. Find a friend who is trying to parent intentionally like you, and the two of you can join forces (and creativity) when it comes to your fun nights.

Connecting with Each Personality

Expressive

Your expressive child longs to laugh with you. Whether you're watching a Ken Davis comedy routine or singing *Silly Songs* along with Larry, the adrenaline rush of laughing (and rolling on the floor gasping, "I can't breathe!") together is immensely bonding.

Analytical

A vital way to connect with your analytical child is to demonstrate sensitivity to her preferences. Make sure that whoever is planning the Fun Night (especially if it's you!) considers your analytical's likes and dislikes.

Driving

Your driving child craves appreciation; he longs to hear how his efforts have affected you. So be specific as you thank him: "Thank you for planning such a great evening. Since you took over, I was able to relax and enjoy myself."

Amiable

You'll connect best with your amiable child by simply hanging out together. No plan. No agenda. No expectations. Watching a movie on the couch with a take-and-bake pizza is a slice of heaven for this child.

Dinner Together

Try This

Eat five meals together with your child this week.

Making the Connection

It sounds so simple, but when a family is balancing work, kids' band practice, the puggle's vet appointments, and church choir rehearsal, your van probably passes beneath the Golden Arches more times than you care to admit. Make it a priority to sit down and eat a meal together at least a few times a week. These can range from dinner at a local restaurant to pancakes and bacon on a school morning to a Saturday tailgate before a big game. Not only is this a time to nourish your bodies with food, you can nourish your family with good conversation and fun.

Focus on the Family's "Make Every Day Count" campaign's web page says "families that share mealtimes at least four times a week see improved communication and healthier eating habits. Children of families who regularly have dinner together also develop a protection factor against all important risk behaviors." The benefits of eating together are hard to argue.

But so are the challenges. I know the thought of trying to wrangle your family to sit at the dinner table four times a week may be a bit overwhelming. You may have squiggly toddlers or sullen teens, and it just seems as if it's not worth the effort. I understand. I've had those exact same feelings.

When Roger and I were first married, we were trying to blend all these kids into one family. At no time was that more awkward than at the family dinner table.

Justen was loud and boisterous, telling us all in great detail about his American history class. Jeremy, who was used to having his dad and his house pretty much to himself, hated that he was forced to sit at the table. And Kimberly? It depended on how things went at school that day. If she and her friend got along, we had Chatty Kimmy. If there had been a slight (real or imagined), we got Grunting Girl.

And as far as the menu? It seemed that this crew wasn't going to be happy with anything I cooked. Until we got married, Roger's go-to strategy for feeding his kids involved ordering dinner through an inter-com. It's hard to compare homemade with the Golden Arches when it comes to a fifteen-year-old's palate.

You can see why I was not exactly approaching the kitchen with a Rachael Ray smile every evening.

Eventually, dinner became easier. As the kids got a little older and I understood the challenges of the dinner table better, we were able to make our time together a little more nurturing and a little less silent.

Make Connecting Fun

Here are some of the things that lead to a better connection through dinner.

Build Your Own Meals

I hated the thought of having a showdown over broccoli several nights a week. Each family has their own clean-plate policy, and I respect that. But for our family, it was more important to lessen the battle at the table for the first couple of years. So a few times a week we required the kids to put together their own meals. Some nights we had top-your-own pita pizzas; other nights it was soup-and-salad bars. Yes, most evenings were take-it-or-leave-it style, but I always looked forward to the dinners when I knew at least the casserole wasn't going to be a point of contention.

When you are doing a "Build Your Own Meal," the key is to have a lot of little containers of food to build with. That way, everyone gets to use their favorites or try something new. Here are some variations on the "build your own meals" theme:

- *Waffle Bar*—Start with waffles. Top with strawberries, blueberries, syrups, jams and jellies, powdered sugar, cinnamon, butter, Nutella, bacon.

- *Salad Bar*—Start with different kinds of washed and torn-up lettuce. Top with cucumbers, tomatoes, broccoli, carrots, peppers, hard boiled eggs, croutons, shredded cheese.

- *Potato Bar*—Start with baked potatoes. Top with sour cream, butter, shredded cheese, steamed broccoli, chili, chicken, bacon, chives.

- *Soup Bar*—Start with one or two soups in bowls. Top with shredded cheese, large croutons, sour cream, crackers, chilies, tortilla strips, oyster crackers, chicken strips, chopped green onions.

- *Taco Bar*—Start with taco shells, tostada shells, or tortillas. Top with cooked, seasoned meats (chicken, pork, ground beef, shredded beef, shrimp), cheeses, beans, sour cream, guacamole, peppers, shredded lettuce, chopped tomatoes, olives.

- *Pita Pizza Bar*—Start with pitas topped with pasta sauce. Top with shredded cheese, pepperoni, turkey pepperoni, purple onions, mushrooms, ham, green peppers, pineapple chunks, sun-dried tomatoes.

- *Grilled Cheese Bar*—Start with bread and cheese (try new cheeses that you wouldn't normally put on your grilled cheese sandwich, such as gruyere or brie, but keep some American on hand for more traditional palates). Top with ham, chicken, tomatoes, grilled onions.

And food bars aren't just for dinner. You can have a great time connecting over something sweet as well:

- *Hot Chocolate Bar*—Start with mugs of hot chocolate. Top with marshmallows, whipped cream, candy canes (as swizzle sticks), coffee flavorings (vanilla or hazelnut syrup), cookies or brownies for dipping.

- *Sundae Bar*—Start with ice cream. Top with syrups, nuts, candies, jimmies, marshmallows, bananas, whipped cream, cherries.

Community Food

My friend and fellow speaker Cheri Gregory has taken "Build Your Own Pizza" night to a new level. Cheri lives on campus at a boarding school where she teaches English to high school students. Since the kids live away from home, they are even more eager to have a home-cooked meal. When Cheri and her husband, Daniel, host a pizza night, it's a sight to behold. They have three breadmakers all going at the same time to create homemade dough to feed their own kids as well as any students that may wander by. Here is Cheri's no-longer-secret recipe for great breadmaker pizza dough:

● ●

Breadmaker Pizza Dough

1 package active dry yeast

1 cup lukewarm water

1 drop of honey

Whisk the yeast and honey into the water and allow yeast to proof. Place the yeast-honey mixture into your breadmaker and then add:

3 cups flour

2 tsp. sugar

2 T. olive oil

1 tsp. salt

Once you've added all the ingredients, hit the "dough" setting. We check five minutes into the "dough" cycle to make sure it's not too stiff. It should be soft and pliable without being sticky.

● ●

Cheri also has three Presto Pizzazz pizza ovens. These countertop pizza bakers look like space-age record players. They actually have a turntable to rotate the pizza so it cooks evenly. You can either precook the pizza in a conventional oven or put it directly on the pizza oven and create your pizza with assorted toppings there.

Why have I gone into elaborate detail about the creation of a pizza? Because it's an opportunity for your family to connect and have fun for longer than it takes to wolf down a bowl of pasta.

Another variation on community food is the simmering-pot dinner. A simmering-pot meal is anything you cook in the middle of the table. Think fondue and you get an idea of what I'm talking about. Yes, this depends on the age of your kids and their ability to handle hot pots and pointy sticks, but it's a great conversation starter, will provide loads of fun, and be memorable for you and your kids.

Here is our family's all-time favorite fondue recipe:

• •

Pizza Fondue
Connie Richerson

½ lb. ground beef

1 small onion, chopped

2 (10.5 oz.) jars pasta sauce

1 T. cornstarch

1½ tsp. oregano

¼ tsp. garlic powder

2 cups cheddar cheese, shredded

1 cup mozzarella cheese, shredded

Brown the ground beef and onion; drain. Put meat, sauce, cornstarch, and spices in fondue pot. When cooked and bubbly, add cheese. Spear crusty French bread cubes, then dip and swirl in fondue. This is also delicious with breadsticks.

Serves 4 to 6.

• •

If your kids are "food adventurous," you may want to try some other simmering-pot ideas that are a little more out there but just as fun. If your kids love cheese and meat, you could look up directions for raclette, which is both a type of cheese and a Swiss dish based on heating the cheese and scraping off (*racler*) the melted part. (Find great information and recipes at www.raclette.com.au.) Or if you want to go with an Asian flair, you could try our favorite Japanese dish, sukiyaki.

Sukiyaki is a popular one-pot meal in Japan that's cooked at the table as you eat. Yaki means "grilled" in Japanese. All these flavors blend together for an incredible meal that's also a ton of fun to eat.

Sukiyaki

1 lb. thinly sliced beef, cut into bite-size pieces

1 package cellophane noodles, washed and drained, cut into 3-inch pieces

8 shiitake mushrooms, stems removed

1 leek, washed and sliced into 2-inch lengths

½ Chinese cabbage, washed and cut

1 14-oz. package yaki-dofu (grilled tofu), cut into bite-size pieces

For sukiyaki sauce:

1/3 c. soy sauce

3 T. sake

5 T. sugar

¾ cup water

For dipping: 4 pasteurized eggs (optional)

Arrange ingredients on a large plate on the dining table. Mix soy sauce, sake, sugar, and water to make the sukiyaki sauce. Set an electric wok or electric skillet on the table. Heat the oil in the wok. Fry some beef slices and then pour the sukiyaki sauce into the wok. When the sauce starts to boil, place the other ingredients in the wok and turn down the heat to "simmer." Simmer until all ingredients are softened. You can dip the cooked meat and veggies into the raw egg, as is tradition in Japan. But if the thought of serving raw eggs to your kids makes you uneasy, skip that step. It's delicious without them.

Serves 4.

On Location

It's funny how a meal served at the dinner table can be an ordeal, but the exact same food served in the backyard can turn into an event.

During the months with the fairest weather, we eat about half our dinners outside on our postage-stamp-sized patio. There is something magical about the change of location that makes a meal into a moment.

And this isn't just for home. Are you driving from band practice to soccer practice with just enough time to drive through your favorite (or not so favorite) burger joint? Hey, it happens to all of us. But instead of wolfing down your dinner on the drive, why not wait until you get to your destination, pull out a blanket, and make an instant picnic of it?

We've had carpet picnics in the middle of the living room, real picnics at a park, and stuffed-animal picnics in a kid's room.

This past Christmas, we loaded all our kids in our minivan and had a Drive-Thru Dinner and Christmas Lights night. We googled "the best Christmas lights in San Jose" and put all the addresses into Mapquest.com. MapQuest came up with the best route for us to take, a big circle starting with and ending with our house. Along the way, we drove through In-N-Out Burger for dinner, and toward the end of the night, drove through Starbucks for a small hot chocolate. The only time we got out of the car the entire evening was to drop donations into the Make-A-Wish collection centers that some of the more over-the-top decorated houses featured. It was a great night, and the kids asked if we could do it again next year. While I wouldn't want to have seven people eating burgers in my car every night, for a once-a-year treat, it was a blast.

Make Connecting Work

Make It a Nag-Free Zone

It's easy to want to follow up on homework at the kitchen table. Everyone is sitting right there and it just makes sense. Resist the temptation. I remember the conversations that we would have when the topic turned (by me) to homework.

Me: "How was your day?"

Grunting child: "Fine."

Me: "Do you have homework?"

Grunting child: "No."

Me (in my head): *Liar.*

Use this time instead to focus on connecting. In another chapter, we're going to talk about Dinnertime Conversation Starters—ways to keep the dinner talk up and interesting. Save the homework and chore chat for a different time of day.

Be Our Guest

Have you ever noticed that when you invite a friend to dinner (whether it's one of your kid's friends or one of yours), the conversation goes in new directions, and you find out things about your kids you never would have known? Your kids will open up in areas that they may not be willing to share with you. Invite someone over and see your kids in a new light.

Teen Challenges

Friend and author Elizabeth Thompson gives this advice about teens and the dinner table:

> "When attempting to connect with teens, remember your goal: connection. If your goal is to change them (behavior, thinking, etc.) you'll come across as critical. Your teen will feel rejected and become defensive or distant. If we meet our kiddos where they are (connecting with them), we can then lead them to where we want them to go. The best way to connect at the dinner table or anywhere is to *listen.* As parents we want to be heard, and we should be. But our teens want to be heard too."

> "We told our teens—and their friends—they could talk about or ask questions about anything, as long as they were not vulgar or unkind. Wow! Some of the questions sent my husband, Mike, to the other room!"—Dana

Try This at Home

"I would sometimes surprise my teens with candles on the table, lights low, and my china. They'd come rolling in after football practice or whatever and say, 'Who's coming over for dinner?' (I think they secretly hoped it meant pizza in their room.) I'd tell them, 'You are!' They'd roll their eyes, but when it was time to eat they had cleaned up a bit. We prayed, and then I told them each how much I loved them (husband too) and how honored I was to be their mom (wife). I brought up funny stories from when they were younger, and we all laughed. As the dinner rolled on, I finally asked if there was a certain area where they wished I could be more available for them. It opened the door for all kinds of sharing. I just had to keep my mouth shut and let them have the floor."—Mimi Moseley

Step It Up

If you're struggling as a blended family, keep the dinner table a safe zone. Ask open-ended questions and don't judge the answers. We found that when we had a consistent dinnertime, it made it easier on the whole family to plan their evenings and there weren't as many struggles to get people to the table.

Suggestions for Singles

I asked my friend Jill what steps she took to overcome some of the dinner-time drama as a single mom:

"Connecting over dinner has always been important to me from the very beginning of being a mom. I would spend time preparing, and then enjoy the time together. I homeschooled, and we ate three meals a day together, but somehow dinner was special. Even though my husband was often not home (Air Force pilot), dinnertime was the signal of the homeschool day being over and just family time.

"I loved the book by Gloria Gaither and Shirley Dobson called *Let's Make a Memory*, about family traditions and dinner. I would do all the things they recommended. We had a special plate for a special person to celebrate, we would do dinner by candlelight, each kid would get to choose a special meal, and I had notecards with conversation starters on them.

"And then I got divorced. And dinner was the last thing I wanted to even think about.

"I finally realized that it was not actually dinner I hated; it was deciding what to make. And I knew as a single parent, it was more important than ever that I get dinner on the table. I had spent years as a proponent of once-a-month cooking, even speaking to MOPS groups about freezer cooking. Now newly single, it was just too daunting for me with all the other changes in my life.

"For the first couple of years, drive-thru was my friend, even though I knew it was too expensive for my budget. Then the economic downturn hit, and I knew I had to cut it out.

"I brainstormed with my kids about what they wanted. They are, much to my dismay, picky eaters, and I do not have enough energy to change that. So we had to figure out a way for them to get fed, me to not feel guilty about feeding them too many processed foods, and still make it easy and food they wanted. They put together our meal wheel. There are seven meals on it. I keep the ingredients for the seven meals on hand, and we spin to decide what to have for dinner. I don't have to think about it, it's easy, and I have energy to talk at dinner.

"Recently they've started to like salad, so salad fixings are always in the fridge. I go shopping at our local healthy food store and buy veggies once a week, cut them up, and put them in Baggies with a paper towel to absorb moisture. Now we can always add a salad to dinner in a flash."

Connecting with Each Personality

Expressive

For your expressive child, family mealtime is a chance to talk...and talk and talk some more! You can channel this chatter energy. Get him excited about playing MC for the evening, asking questions of the rest of the group and learning to listen in between.

Analytical

Your analytical child thrives on precision. Encourage her to learn the "official" way to set the table. Let her be the expert on the correct placement of knives and the right time to use each fork. If you want to make her week, let her help plan precise menus with you.

Driving

This child loves to be in charge. Invite him to make place cards for everyone, to determine the seating arrangement, to serve the food, and to make the all-important announcement: "Dinner is served!"

Amiable

Don't rush your amiable child through the meal. Allow plenty of time and space for her to relax and enjoy connecting with other family members.

Connection
3

Looking for the Positive

Try This

Fill the conversations you have with your kids with encouragement.

Making the Connection

When Roger and I got married, we had a protester at our wedding. He wasn't carrying any signs, chanting, or tying himself to trees, but no one who was at our poolside nuptials could have missed his message. Roger's son, Jeremy, did *not* want this wedding to happen.

Jeremy had liked me, until he found out his dad liked me. Then, all of a sudden, I was public enemy number one.

Roger and I naively thought that if we just loved him enough and gave him a stable home, he would come around. But Jeremy was firm. He did not approve of our marriage, and he did not approve of me.

It was an incredibly hard situation. With Jeremy and my kids living with Roger and me full time, there never seemed to be a break from the drama. It was exhausting, saddening, and downright maddening.

Roger and I went to a counselor to see how we could live in peace. The first thing we learned in counseling was that whatever happened, the best thing we could do for Jeremy was to have a strong marriage. The next thing I realized was that Jeremy was a kid who needed and craved encouragement. His dad was great at it. Me? Not so much. Let's face it; it's hard to encourage someone when you feel as though they've made it their mission to make your life miserable.

This was about the time I was writing *The Husband Project*, a book all about loving your husband on purpose. I realized I needed to do the same thing for the other men in my life. My boys.

So I set about to encourage each of them, once a day, for three weeks. I would compliment Jeremy on a chore he did or on the way he ran track that day. I worked hard to look for the good in him wherever I could find it.

That was about four years ago, and Jeremy and I have a different relationship today. I look forward to having him over for dinner and hanging out. I love seeing the man he is becoming. I don't know how much of an impact those words of encouragement had on him, but they made a world of difference to me. Instead of focusing on Jeremy's bad attitude, I focused on all the great attributes he had.

Make Connecting Fun

You love your kids. A lot. So you'd think it'd be easy to be their biggest cheerleader and encourage them with every step they take. But then they get tired and cranky. And then you get tired and cranky. And suddenly "You're amazing!" turns into "It'd be amazing if you went and played your guitar in the other room for a while."

Here are six easy ways—compliments of my friend and encouragement mentor Kimberly Gonsalves (www.parenting4thelongrun.com)—to shower your kids with encouragement today.

Schedule special time with each of your kids. Let them know that you'd like to spend time with just them and brainstorm some activities that both of you enjoy. For younger children, even ten minutes a day is great. This is time when you're present, not multitasking. It can be as simple as playing a game, going for a walk, reading, having milk and cookies together, or just snuggling and playing on the floor. For school-age children and older, thirty minutes a week that they can count on will help keep that connection strong even as they head into adolescence. Teens still need time with you too (although you'll be competing with friends and extracurricular activities), and listening, humor, curiosity, and appreciation are skills you'll need to use (or develop) if you want them to open up. Some is better than none. Start where you can.

Tell your child what you notice and love about them...often. My son is becoming so mature when it comes to apologizing and making amends. I've shared with him how much I admire his honesty in taking responsibility for his actions and his willingness to try again. He's also funny and creative. My daughter is usually willing to try just about anything, and I love her sense of adventure. She's also kind. Make it a point to tell them something every single day that you love about them.

Let your child teach you something. Do you have any idea how hard it is to ride a ripstick? Learn the hottest playground game or the millennial version of pat-a-cake. Need an IT person? Look no further than your ten-year-old. Ask your child to teach you to play their favorite game on the Wii or other video game. Be prepared to be humbled! Choose something your child enjoys and is good at, and learn how to be a beginner again.

Invent something new together. On Thanksgiving a few years back, I was giving my kids the old line about "when I was a kid, no one set up play dates for us! We used to play together in the street and entertain ourselves with all kinds of things we found lying around."

Not long after, we found a cardboard tube, about five feet long, in the neighbor's recycling bin. We invented a new game called "garbage ball," which combines running, throwing, and dribbling skills. While running down the street dribbling a soccer ball, the first person would swipe the cardboard tube at the ball (think field hockey) to pass it to the next person, then toss the cardboard tube to them on the run, at which point they had to make contact with the ball the same way, passing it and the tube to someone else. My kids were seven and eleven at the time, and we were quite a sight!

You might make up a crazy song together or write a poem.

Help them find ways they can share their skills and talents. Is your child highly organized and attentive to detail? Maybe you know someone looking for some office help. If your child likes to cook, see if they'd like to prepare a meal once a week or volunteer to take meals to the sick, if your church does that. If your child is a strong student, check into tutoring opportunities for them. With your child's permission, share their talents. Hearing that their skills and contributions are valued carries extra oomph for your kids when it comes from someone other than their parents.

Lighten up. Humor can be a huge encouragement. Irony, metaphor, gentle teasing with love, even self-deprecating humor can be ways to connect. We have some inside jokes about our flaws: "we're off like a herd of turtles!" when we finally manage to load everyone in and pull out of the driveway; tolerance for personal style preferences (eschewing the use of hairbrushes during certain developmental stages); those of us that fall prey to "bright, shiny object syndrome."

Make Connecting Work

Kimberly, my encouragement mentor, is a bona fide parenting coach (read more about her work at www.parenting4thelongrun.com), which means she knows a *lot* about encouraging kids. She's also shared with me some of her best tips on how to make sure your efforts at encouragement don't fall flat. Here they are:

Make time, even when it's inconvenient. When you were growing up, who made you feel loved? Special? Worthy of time and attention? Normal? On occasion, my dad would make himself available as a listening ear if I needed to talk. A few times, he even went to work late. I remember feeling so loved and thinking that I must be so important to him.

Unplug. Set some boundaries around your own use of electronics in your home, times when you will be mentally present and available for interaction. It's hard to connect when you can't even get someone to acknowledge you or look up from what they're doing. This might need to be combined with humor or exaggeration to make it go down easier if you have let technology run amok in the past.

Ask for their opinion. And listen. Get curious and see how much you can learn. No lecturing!

Share their interests. Try snowboarding, listen to their music, explore the thrill of paintball, cook together, read the same book, or watch their favorite TV show together. Even if your taste is different (shocker, huh?), you can still have fun together visiting their world.

Be respectful. If your default style of relating to your child would kill your adult friendships, think about making some changes.

Acknowledge your kids' strengths and help them build on them. "Everybody is a genius. But if you judge a fish by its ability to climb a tree, it will live its whole life believing that it is stupid"—Albert Einstein.

Treat mistakes as opportunities to learn. When your child blows it, don't hammer them with their mistake. Be curious about what their perspective is. Many times our kids know they've made a mistake and don't need us to point it out to them. (Do you like having someone point out your mistakes to you?) Ask what they learned from the situation. What might they do differently next time? Is it something you need to give them more practice with? Thomas Edison said, "I have not failed. I have just found 10,000 ways that won't work." (Personally, I admit to hoping for a number that's smaller than 10,000. But then, I haven't invented a new technology.)

Celebrate progress. We can all use someone on our side to help us remember how far we've come.

Celebrate effort, not just outcome. Most of us need repeated practice to master anything. Notice effort, perseverance, sticking with it, and not giving up. As kids get older, they become quite aware of how they stack up against others. Celebrating effort and noticing improvement, even when they haven't been completely successful at something, might be just the thing that helps them hang in there until they reach their goal.

Listen. With busy schedules and multitasking becoming more and more prevalent, be conscious about really listening to your child.

Be curious. Ask for your child's opinion on something. Then listen. Instead of arguing or trying to persuade them to your point of view, be curious and ask questions without an agenda. What evidence have you seen for that? What made you notice that? How do you feel about it? What do you think? Is there anything else you want to say? You'll get a bit of insight into their view of the world. It can be tempting to lecture or negate what they're saying, but try to just listen and learn.

Validate feelings. Show your child you are listening and that you understand by validating their feelings. "You think your math teacher doesn't like you." This doesn't mean you agree with or condone everything they say, but it provides a way for them to feel understood. "You

were embarrassed when he called on you and you didn't know the answer."
Where appropriate, you might share a similar experience you had. "I
think I can understand how you feel. I had a similar experience when…"

Cast your child in a positive light. Think about the qualities that may
drive you nuts about your child: impatient, argumentative, aggressive,
demanding, overly sensitive, does the bare minimum required to get by.
Then picture a time when you were really enjoying yourself with your
child (perhaps when they were asleep!). Now, with this image in mind,
turn those negatives into the positive traits that will shine through in
adulthood:

- *impatient* might become *leader*

- *aggressive* might become *focused*

- *demanding* may be *persuasive*

- *argumentative* might be *able to persevere when challenged*

- *overly sensitive* might be *empathic* or *attuned*

- *does the bare minimum* might become *efficient, clear priorities*

Understand your child's temperament. Understand temperament and
know it's not right or wrong, it just is. Introverted, extroverted, slow
to warm up or quick to jump in? Quickly overwhelmed by noise or
crowds? Working with your child's basic temperament can mean giving shy children time to adjust to new people or situations instead of
pushing them to participate right away or shaming them.

At the same time, you can help them by recounting times when
they were tentative about a new activity, and then recalling the steps
they took to join the group and how much fun they ended up having.
With children who have lots of energy and feed on social experiences,
help them meet that need by arranging for them to be with others. This
also prevents you from having to be the sole source of interactions. You
can balance that by helping them learn to enjoy periods of solitude,
since all of us need to learn how to be alone. Don't forget to take your
own temperament and needs into account as well.

Apologize when you're in the wrong. There's a lot of correcting to be done as a parent, and sometimes we overdo it. When you can admit your mistakes, offer a genuine apology, and make amends (taking some action to restore the relationship, if necessary), it's very encouraging to a child. It also is a powerful way to model the skills they'll need in life.

Acknowledge without words. A knowing smile, a hug, a pat on the back, a thumbs-up, a corny victory dance, can all be ways to encourage without ever opening your mouth.

A Little Something Extra

We all love our kids, but sometimes it's harder to think of ways to encourage them than others. Here are fifty ideas from some of my favorite parents on things you can say to encourage your child today.

50 things you can say to encourage your kids right now

1. I'm so glad that Jesus trusted me with you.
2. I believe in you.
3. I will always love you...no matter what.
4. Please forgive me.
5. God's love for you will never change.
6. I love watching your gift of generosity (or hospitality or encouragement) in action.
7. You have a great sense of humor.
8. I am so glad to be your mother/father.
9. I love spending time with you.
10. I'm proud of you.
11. You are fun to be with.
12. You are such a good person.
13. You make my heart happy.
14. Just being you is always enough.

15. You are an important part of *His*tory.

16. You make me laugh.

17. I'm glad you're my son.

18. I'm glad you're my daughter.

19. You make me feel special.

20. You are so creative!

21. That was a wise decision.

22. I loved you before I met you.

23. I see kindness in the way you treat others.

24. Your tender heart encourages me.

25. You make me a better person.

26. You're the best gift I ever received.

27. I love the person God created you to be.

28. You make me want to wake up in the morning.

29. You are my miracle.

30. You are a perfect fit for our family.

31. God is really turning you into something special.

32. You teach me so much about _____ (Legos, photography, science, fashion).

33. I couldn't do _____ without you.

34. You can do this.

35. You make me happy.

36. You do that really well.

37. God will be by your side no matter what.

38. Your smile is contagious.

39. You're so important to me.

40. I'm thankful for you in my life.

41. You're a good friend.

42. You're a good brother.

43. You're a good sister.

44. I don't care what we do today as long as I can be with you.

45. Let me help you.

46. You're so good at solving problems.

47. I love your compassionate spirit.

48. I will never stop loving you.

49. I pray for you every day.

50. God created you exactly how he wanted you.

Teen Challenges

This time I really do have a challenge for you. In their book *Positive Discipline for Teenagers: Empowering Your Teen and Yourself Through Kind and Firm Parenting*, authors Jane Nelsen and Lynn Lott challenge parents of teenagers to do one simple thing: Spend at least five minutes a day with their teenager while keeping

1. their mouth shut (listening)

2. their sense of humor intact (perspective)

3. their ears open (curiosity)

4. their heart emanating warmth and gratitude (love)

5. a desire to understand their teen's world (focusing)

So simple in theory, yet so hard in practice.

Step It Up

Roger and I found that when corrections needed to happen for one of our kids, it was vital that it wasn't from the stepparent. My job was to be the encourager.

Look—really hard—for things to encourage your stepchild with.

Suggestions for Singles

For my friend Jill, who is single and raising kids, using encouraging words is a very important part of her life:

> I really began to discover the power of positive words about sixteen years ago, and it has carried me a long way in connecting with my children.
>
> In my home of origin, positive, encouraging words were few and far between. Although I tried to be positive with my kids (and I think I did an adequate job), I didn't really know how to, since it had never been modeled for me.
>
> It was about this time my mom went to hear Florence Littauer speak on her book titled *Silver Boxes: The Gift of Encouragement*. My mother bought me a copy of the book with a little silver box that contained a beautiful pair of diamond earrings. She hugged me and told me she realized how hurtful her words had been. This was the beginning of my healing as well as my journey to speak encouragement to my children.
>
> As a single parent I have had to become more intentional about providing those positive and encouraging words. A few ways that I make sure to use positive words:
>
> I don't say "I can't believe you did that," or "What were you thinking?" My comment instead is "Wow, honey, that is so not like you. What happened?" This takes away the condemnation and judgment, helps them to not become defensive, and allows them a place to discuss how to handle that situation differently if it or a similar situation comes up again.
>
> Another thing I do with my children is to use positive affirmations. A few years ago Gracie was in the middle of a bullying situation and just getting out of the car for school was an everyday challenge. So we put together a deck of positive affirmation cards, and every day she would pull one

in the morning, and then when I picked her up, we would discuss how it helped her to focus on the good in her world that day.

I try to offer a positive spin when encouraging my children to look at the positive, but there are times they tell me, "Mom, I just need you to listen. Please don't coach me on this." My children are smart. And so I have had to learn at times to just listen.

The biggest challenge I have in this area is to keep the words of encouragement going when my kids come home from visiting their dad. Our divorce was an extremely bitter one, and there is still a lot of hurt as well as a lot of healing that needs to happen. Even though I want to agree with my kids about how lousy their dad may have been or what awful things he has said, I work hard to encourage them to turn around his negative input.

For example, my son had major difficulty spelling when he started fourth grade. We developed a saying that he repeated every day and multiple times before a spelling test: "I always get 100 percent on my spelling tests." His dad told him this was stupid because he couldn't possibly get 100 percent since he was so bad at spelling. I had to both encourage Jacob and keep from saying anything bad about his dad. The good news is that although in fourth grade he didn't ever get 100 percent on a spelling test, now in ninth grade he is a 4.0 student. I believe that if I had put his dad down at that point, it would have erased all the good I had done. Jacob learned a valuable lesson.

Connecting with Each Personality

Expressive

Because your expressive child craves approval, his primary love language is *words of affirmation*. When a positive thought about him crosses your mind, *say it aloud*. Don't worry about going overboard; your "too much" is his "just about right."

Analytical

Your analytical child may seem serious, even a bit down in the dumps. You'll connect deeply with her by quietly expressing your support in whatever she's experiencing rather than trying to cheer her up or get her to snap out of it.

Driving

No matter how challenging your driving child acts, you can ask an open-ended question such as, "What would I ever do without you?" to express gratitude. Don't be surprised if you receive in reply a confident, "I have absolutely no idea!"

Amiable

Nothing frustrates an amiable child quite like discussing her potential. She hears this as an accusation of laziness and a demand to earn encouragement or approval. She needs to hear that she's OK—that you love her just the way she is.

Connection
4

Home, a Safe Place to Land

Try This

Take some simple steps to make your home a safe place for your kids to go whenever they need support, friendship, a shoulder to cry on, or someone to celebrate with.

Making the Connection

Is your home a safe haven for your kids?

I confess there were several years when mine wasn't. Looking back, I wish I had done things differently. When my kids were in elementary school, our house was not so much a home as a dumping ground (backpacks, shoes, sweatshirts), filling station (food, juice, water), and a drive-thru kid wash.

I couldn't really say that my heart was at home. My heart was really in my minivan.

The kids' school was on the other side of town and so was our church. Many days it didn't make sense to go all the way home between school and church activities, so we wouldn't make it back home until later in the evening, all in time to get to bed and repeat the whole thing the next day.

That's no way to provide a peaceful home.

Now that I've had a few more years of being a parent, I realize that no one is going to revoke my mom card for not having my kids in every activity that our local YMCA offers. Over the next few years I worked hard to keep our life as home-centric as possible. It was important for me to help my kids pursue their passions, but I also realized it wasn't a federal mandate to have my kids in soccer.

So what does having a soft place to land for your kids look like?

I think that the key word is *peace*. When you look up a definition of peace, a common phrase is "a freedom from disturbance." I love that definition as a goal for our homes.

Here's a way to figure out the "peace level" of your home. Ask yourself, *How do I feel when I walk through the front door?* We've all heard the saying, "When momma ain't happy, ain't nobody happy." If you're not at peace when you come through the door, my guess is that no one in your house is either. I want you to feel at peace so that your family will be at peace. I want your house to be a soft place to land for you so that will overflow to the rest of your family.

It can feel impossible with work and home and kids and schedules. But I want you to spend a little time thinking about how you can create some space in your home for yourself, as well as your kids. Here are just a few suggestions.

Make Connecting Fun

The good news here is that it's not hard to make your home a safe place to land. It really just takes a little time, a little ingenuity, and a listening ear. Here are some simple tips on how to make it happen.

Break for Coffee

After a long day at school, my kids needed a chance to unwind before diving into their history and algebra homework. Once they'd had a chance to pet the dog and put away their backpacks, we would gather around the kitchen table and have our after-school coffee break. We'd have popcorn and hot chocolate, cookies with a tall glass of frosty milk, or pretzels and lemonade. This is when I would find out about the day's happenings at school, how much homework there was for the evening, and, most importantly, how I could pray for my kids while they were at school.

To have your own coffee break, all you need to do is prepare a simple snack and be ready to ask open-ended questions. Instead of "How was your day?" ask, "What did you and Haley talk about at recess this morning?" or "I know you studied really hard for your chemistry test. Was it as tough as you thought it would be?" Try to stay focused on your kids during this time. Look at them, listen to their stories no matter how convoluted they get, and make sure you share a little about your day as well.

Some kids just need to decompress after school and don't feel like replaying their day right away. For other families, it might be nearly dinnertime before everyone is home. The point of the coffee break isn't to add more stress to your lives but to give you a regular time to talk through the day. So fit your coffee break in where it works best for you and your children.

Turn Your House into a House of Prayer

If you want peace in your home, the number one way of making that happen is to pray for it. Here are some of my favorite verses to not only meditate on but to pray for when it comes to peace:

> "Come to me, all you who are weary and burdened, and I will give you rest. Take my yoke upon you and learn from me, for I am gentle and humble in heart, and you will find rest for your souls. For my yoke is easy and my burden is light" (Matthew 11:28-30).

> "Peace I leave with you; my peace I give you. I do not give to you as the world gives. Do not let your hearts be troubled and do not be afraid" (John 14:27).

> "I have told you these things, so that in me you may have peace. In this world you will have trouble. But take heart! I have overcome the world" (John 16:33).

> Let the peace of Christ rule in your hearts, since as members of one body you were called to peace. And be thankful (Colossians 3:15).

"The LORD bless you
>and keep you;
>the LORD make his face shine on you
>and be gracious to you;
>the LORD turn his face toward you
>and give you peace"
>(Numbers 6:25-26).

Make Your Walls Talk

I'm a big believer in letting your walls do your talking. If a peaceful home is something you're striving for, place some of the verses above in prominent places. Whether you write verses on vinyl stickers placed on the window above your kitchen sink or frame one of those verses inside a garage-sale picture frame that you've painted black and hung by the front door, having a reminder of how God intended you to live is a powerful way to change the temperature of your home.

Add a Few Creature Comforts

While the emotional and spiritual comfort of your home is key, let's not forget a few physical comforts as well.

Every person in your home should have a space that is all their own. Maybe it's just a bed lounger (a pillow backrest for their bed) on the bottom bunk or a bean bag in the corner of a room they share with their little sister, but it's a little corner of the world that is all for them. Everyone should have a quiet place that is all their own where they can escape from the rest of the world and curl up with a good book, a blanket, and their thoughts.

Ban the Stress

Think about the times of the day that are overwhelming for you and your kids…and then come up with solutions for how to ban the stress from that time. For my family, the high-stress time is always getting ready in the morning. Our solution? We prep the night before.

After I got tired of playing "Hunt the Nike" every day for two weeks (and showing up late to work because of it), I made a plan to do as much as I can the night before so that our path out the door wasn't riddled with potholes. It worked.

Now one of our favorite sayings is "Getting out the door is all about the night before." Here is a list of getting-out-the-door prep steps from my book *The Get Yourself Organized Project*:

The Night Before

1. Check backpacks and make sure everything your child's teacher is expecting to show up is in there.
2. Pack lunches.
3. Set out clothes for you and your kids.
4. Place backpacks, purses, and briefcases by the front door.
5. Charge cell phones.
6. Make sure your gas tanks contain gas.
7. Move anything that needs to be defrosted for tomorrow night's dinner from the freezer to the fridge.
8. Set up coffeemaker with water and grounds.
9. Set out cereal bowls, dishes, and glasses for breakfast.
10. Set out your Thermos and water bottles (or chill water bottles in the fridge).
11. Charge your laptop.
12. Set alarm clocks.
13. Place keys where you can find them.
14. Empty the dishwasher so the morning dishes can go directly into it.
15. Shut off your computer at least an hour before you plan to go to bed. Your brain needs some transition time.
16. Go to bed on time.

The Morning Of

1. Stagger bathroom times if you have multiple people using the same bathroom.

2. If you have a half bath in another part of the house, one
   child can use that for everything but the shower.

If you find yourself starting your day by screaming your kids into
the minivan, these hints will help you greatly in experiencing a little
peace in the morning.

Make Connecting Work

So, how exactly do you make your home a safe place to land? My
friend Mary DeMuth says it so eloquently. I've adapted the following
from Mary's excellent book *You Can Raise Courageous and Confident
Kids* (Eugene, OR: Harvest House Publishers, 2007), pages 87-99.

10 Ways to Make Your Home a Haven

The following are ten ways to make your home a haven in this shift-
ing world.

1. *By letting kindness reign.* Determine to treat your children
   and spouse with the same sweetness you'd give a stranger
   you're trying to impress. Remember it's God's kindness
   that leads us to repentance. What makes us think anything
   different would evoke our children's repentance?

2. *By welcoming hard questions.* It's okay to question.
   You did it, didn't you? Give your children the same
   leeway. Let them vent. Let them worry. Welcome their
   wrestling. Don't give pat answers; instead, let them work
   through their questions. Love them through a period of
   questioning.

3. *By being there.* Give your children the rare gift of your
   focused attention. Look into their eyes. Ask great
   questions. Relax alongside them. Dr. Ross Campbell says,
   "In short, focused attention makes a child feel he is the
   most important person in the world in his parents' eyes."

4. *By limiting media.* Steer your children away from mindless
   interaction with the TV or video games. Set limits and

stick to them. Dare to believe your children are creative, innovative kids who can create instead of idly recreate.

5. *By playing outside.* We've lost the importance of outdoor play. Even if it means walking to the park with your kids or swimming alongside them or taking a nature hike, dare to move beyond the four walls of your home to venture out to see God's creation.

6. *By weeping and rejoicing at the right times.* We are to weep with those who weep and rejoice with those who rejoice (Romans 12:15). When a child has a difficult day, scoop her into your arms and cry alongside. When she makes a great grade, jump up and down and celebrate with ice cream.

7. *By cherishing childhood.* Our kids grow up so fast in this crazy culture. Keep them kids as long as you can. Let them play, run, stretch, linger. Limit activities when they're younger so they don't become little stressed-out adults at age ten.

8. *By reading together.* The most haven-producing thing I do as a mommy is simply to read to my kids. I still read to my fourteen year old! Discover audiobooks as a family, lessening the tedium of car rides without popping in a DVD. My kids have stayed in the car to listen to a story finish.

9. *By laughing hard, but not at* another's *expense.* Joking and laughter are blessings you can add to create a fun-loving haven, but be cautious not to laugh at your kids' expense or allow them to laugh at yours or others' expense. Watch funny, clean movies together. Tell jokes. Tell funny family stories over and over until they become ridiculous. A lighthearted family that doesn't take itself too seriously is a haven-home.

10. *By practicing God's presence in the mundane.* Require chores of your kids. It teaches them important life skills. Even so,

introduce joy as you work. Turn on the radio, dance, laugh. By learning to practice the presence of God during the chores of life, you create a productive, gratitude-based home.

Teen Challenges

I think it's worth the time and investment to make sure that your teens have a few things that make home a great place to come home to and invite their friends to.

For our brood (at one time we had four teens ages thirteen to eighteen), we got a large-screen TV (OK, some of the reason may have been Roger, but I digress), a Wii, and a pantry with some quick and easy food to prepare. While much was expected of our teens, we wanted them to know that they and their friends were important to us, and we showed that by having a few creature comforts.

For years my son would have a bunch of friends over every Sunday afternoon. They would play games, eat, and hang out. While it wasn't conducive to Roger's Sunday nap, he gave up sleep knowing how much it meant to Justen that his friends wanted to hang out at our home.

Step It Up

We had three kids (two mine, one Roger's) under our 1200-square-foot roof at one time. Talk about some stress.

While we encouraged family togetherness, we also gave everyone some space. Sometimes dinner together meant dinner while watching *Mystery Science Theater 3000*. Yes, dinner together is important, but there are situations when not-so-much bonding is OK.

Suggestions for Singles

Where is your safe place to land? Do you have a little corner of the world so when it's your chance to relax, you can do it?

When I was a single mom, we were living at my parents' house. They had three bedrooms besides their own and offered them all to us. However, I knew that would mean that my mom would have to give up her quilting room, one of those activities that brings her a lot of joy, so I said I would be happy to share a room with my daughter. Kimber was at an age where that wasn't the worst fate in the world, and for the most part, it worked out for me as well.

However, the one thing I needed to be strict about was making sure that Kimber went to bed at a decent time. Not just so she would stay awake during her English class the next morning, but also so I would have some space to be alone and regroup.

Make sure you have a spot in your home that is all yours—a place where you can keep your Bible, a book, a notepad, as well as a spot for a hot cup of tea. As a single parent, you, more than anyone, need a place to relax and recharge.

Connecting with Each Personality

Expressive

While some personalities crave their own corner of the home, your expressive child wants to be in the thick of the action. She may stall at bedtime, so afraid is she of missing all the fun that's sure to happen if she falls asleep before everyone else.

Analytical

Your analytical child needs order; he can't rest if things are in disarray. Create a spot in your home that is all his to organize to his heart's content—where he doesn't have to worry about a little brother coming along and messing up his stuff.

Driving

Modeling wise *energy* management is a vital connection when parenting a driving child. By watching you say no, he will learn that just because he *can* do something doesn't mean he *should*. Seeing you push *pause* will help him learn the value of downtime.

Amiable

A crammed calendar equals a *dis*tressed amiable child. A cleared calendar, a *de*stressed one. No matter how good, true, or noble the activities, for this child the best place to go is nowhere but home.

Connection

5

It's Family Project Time

Try This

Do a family project together.

Making the Connection

Sometimes, we don't give our kids enough credit. We treat our kids like kids because, well, that's what they are. But I'm amazed when I ask my kids to chip in on some grown-up responsibilities, how often they step to the plate.

I remember waking up one Saturday morning a few years ago with a mile-long to-do list whirring around in my brain. I had a church musical on Sunday and had to finish the costumes and the set, plus the cupboards were bare, I hadn't cooked a real meal in two weeks, the house was a mess, and I couldn't even find a ten-minute window to brew myself a cup of coffee.

I worked myself into a panic, trying to figure out if I could manage a 7:00 a.m. run to the grocery store while simultaneously printing out programs and calling the cast with last minute questions. And then I remembered. I had kids. And they were fully (OK, mostly) competent members of our household entirely capable of helping.

Fast forward three hours and I had fully stocked cupboards, a clean-ish house, and a roast in the slow cooker waiting for us when we got home from the church. How did I manage, you might ask? I challenged my kids to a "Get Our Lives in Order" contest, and as a family, we designated tasks, cleaned, cooked, and shopped our way through the mess. I went into Sunday's musical relaxed and ready—and my kids even admitted that they had (a little bit of) fun helping out.

Family projects are not only a great way to get some much-needed items checked off your to-do list, but also an opportunity to interact with your kids in a new way. So start thinking about some things you want to get done and look at them as an opportunity to connect with your kids, to help your home run more smoothly, and even to teach your kids some necessary skills that will serve them well when they are older.

Make Connecting Fun

Here are a few of my favorite family project ideas.

Prepare an Emergency Kit

We live in Northern California where there is no worry of flood or tornados. However, after living here most of my life, earthquakes are not so much of an "if" as a "when." After seeing the real damage that the 1989 quake took on my community, our family would be crazy not to have an emergency kit at the ready.

But wherever you live, you should have an emergency kit. And it is totally appropriate for your kids to be included in putting it together. That way, when an emergency comes, you've already discussed as a family how you are prepared to handle it.

Here is a list from www.72hours.org (a website with a ton of other great resources) of what your basic emergency kit should include:

- Water—one gallon per person per day
- Food—ready to eat or requiring minimal water
- Manual can opener and other cooking supplies
- Plates, utensils, and other feeding supplies
- First-aid kit and instructions
- A copy of important documents and phone numbers

- Warm clothes and rain gear for each family member
- Heavy work gloves
- Disposable camera
- Unscented liquid household bleach and an eyedropper for water purification
- Personal hygiene items, including toilet paper, feminine supplies, hand sanitizer, and soap
- Plastic sheeting, duct tape, and utility knife for covering broken windows
- Tools such as a crowbar, hammer and nails, staple gun, adjustable wrench, and bungee cords
- Blanket or sleeping bag
- Large heavy-duty plastic bags and a plastic bucket for waste and sanitation
- Any special-needs items for children, seniors, or people with disabilities. Don't forget water and supplies for your pets.

Hold a Garage Sale (and bring out your child's inner entrepreneur)

Here's a no-fail, step-by-step strategy to make it work.

1. Strategize

First, sit down with your family and talk about the possibility of a yard sale. Would they be willing participants? Do they have old clothes, toys, or books they could donate to the sale? I've found that it's easier to get buy-in from the whole family if you have a common goal in mind. Perhaps you're looking to save for a family vacation or want to purchase a play set for the backyard. Kids can understand that they have an opportunity to contribute to the home when they realize that they can be a part of those plans happening.

2. Plan

Next, put a date on the calendar for at least a month in the future to hold the sale. This gives you and your family time to go through closets, drawers, basements, and garages and come up with the items you need.

3. Organize

Start off with some empty boxes in an out of the way place in your home (the garage, the laundry room) and start putting things into the boxes as you come across items you no longer need.

Plan a day to work with your kids in their rooms. If they are waffling about whether to sell an item, encourage them to put it in the garage sale box. If they want to retrieve it and play with it, great. If they never think about it again, then it's probably safe to sell. I can't guarantee that there won't be a change of heart on the day of the sale, but often kids get so excited about the idea of selling something that it's easier to let it go.

As you start to gather more and more items, start sorting things by type (kids clothes, kids shoes, toys, books, household gadgets, DVDs). They will be easier to price and display if they are all together.

I encourage you to start pricing items a few weeks before the sale. It's easy to print off price stickers on your computer's printer, and younger kids will have a great time putting stickers on things.

If your kids are parting with some toys that have a lot of little parts, gather up everything in a resealable plastic bag to keep things together.

Start collecting paper bags for shoppers to take their treasures home in.

4. Advertise

On the web. The best way to know where to advertise is to google "garage sales" or "yard sales" (whatever the common terminology is in your area) and the name of your city. You can see where most people are looking for the information and then announce your sale there. But don't spend a lot of money doing this. Most of your traffic will likely be of the drive-by variety. Be sure to highlight the kinds of things you're selling (tools, kids clothes, furniture, etc.) so you attract the right buyers.

On the street. Signs will most likely be your best means of getting people to your sale. While it's tempting to let your kids do the signs, you should manage the project. Cute is not your objective—readable is. My favorite kind of sign is an arrow shape cut out of neon poster board (think hot pink or neon green) with your cross streets clearly labeled. Kids can definitely be part of the sign-hanging process the night before. Make sure you bring copious amounts of clear packing tape, scissors, string, and even some balloons to attach to the sign.

Your friends. Let your friends know about your sale and even the goal you have in mind. Your kids will have a lot more fun if they know some of the people who are stopping by.

Newspaper. Running a cheap ad in your local newspaper or an online classified service will give you more bites.

5. Merchandise

Before I was an author I was a sales rep in the gift industry, and now as a speaker, I have a book table wherever I go. One thing I've learned in both these roles is the power of merchandising—staging items for sale.

Clothes. You are going to sell a lot more clothes for a lot better prices if you have a garment rack to hang them on. Even a shower rod hung from your roof or garage door is a big help. The next best option is to fold clothes neatly on a table (this is a great option for kids clothes especially). Unless you have a lot of wire hangers you're dying to get rid of, be sure to put up a sign that says "Hangers Not Included."

Books, CDs, DVDs. Drag a bookshelf out of your house as a temporary display and, if you have enough shelf space, place the front covers face out. To keep the shelves looking full, put one of your kids in charge of moving items from the bottom rows to the top as books begin to sell.

Put the wows *up front.* You want items up front that will literally stop traffic. Furniture, tools, and electronics are your best bet for getting hubby to pull the car to the curb.

Group items. It's helpful to have similarly priced items on one table. You can have a dollar table, a fifty-cent table, and so on.

6. Capitalize

When the kids were little I would help them set up a lemonade stand to serve those thirsty shoppers in the summer heat (and for my kids to make a little extra cash). This was great for the kids when they were young. They could still be a part of the action, but they didn't have to negotiate with hagglers. Who is going to dicker over a fifty-cent lemonade?

The only problem was that doing a lemonade stand is as much work as the actual garage sale. Finally, I wised up. For our next garage sale a couple of years later, I went to Costco early in the week and bought sodas and bottled waters. All we had to do was ice the drinks and replenish the supply throughout the day, both of which my kids could do without my help.

The kids were thrilled to see their bank grow, and many of the adults were just as excited to get a cheap soda in the middle of a July day.

7. Improvise

Garage sales aren't rigid. You aren't working for Sam Walton, so things don't have to go a certain way. So if something isn't working, improvise!

- Tired of sorting through piles of trinkets that are really worth nothing? Give them away for free with a purchase. Or set out a free box for people to sort through. Better them than you, right?
- Play some music to encourage people to stay awhile.
- Put out a plate of cookies or some lemonade.

Plant a Garden

For a bit longer-term project, why not plant a garden as a family? In our first garden, we planted zucchini, pumpkins, green onions, tomatoes, peppers, rosemary, and basil. We started with a container garden because we were planting on our back patio. But even if you live on several acres, you may want to consider container gardening when you're planting with kids. Container gardens are easier to control, can be moved around if you need to take advantage of sunlight, and are easier to manage when other creatures want to snack on the lovely salad bar you've planted for them.

Talk with your kids about the kind of vegetables you would like to grow. The more input they have up front, the more excited they will be to participate. I have no problem with steering your kids toward vegetables your family will eat and that are easy to grow.

When I first discussed the garden with Kimberly, she was dead set against tomatoes. She didn't like them on her salad and had no interest in growing them. I had to remind her that some of her favorite foods (spaghetti sauce, pizza sauce, ketchup) were made almost entirely out of tomatoes. She relented and had more fun than anyone watching her tomatoes grow.

To help guide your kids, you may want to grow a theme garden. We've had a salsa garden for years now; here's what goes in it:

- a variety of tomato plants
- peppers
- cilantro
- green onions

Or how about a pizza garden:

- a variety of tomato plants
- onions
- basil
- cilantro
- garlic
- peppers

Varieties of almost every vegetable have been developed for containers. Take the kids to the local garden center and pick the expert's brain about what grows best in your area. They can even help you find the right containers for what you'll need. But from my experience, any pots you have lying around will do. Or if you're really trying to do this on the cheap, you could use those five-gallon plastic buckets bakeries have. Often they will give them to you for free or super cheap.

Make Connecting Work

Here are a few rules of thumb to make sure your family project works.

Do it together. Family projects that kids do alone are called chores. And while chores are a good thing (trust me, I'd never get my floors vacuumed if it weren't for my kids), if your goal is to connect, you have to work on family projects together.

Give yourself enough time. A family project shouldn't be stressful, it should be fun. So don't plan a garage sale two days in advance and don't plan to relandscape your entire four-acre yard in one weekend.

Let your kids help plan. Let your kids be involved in every step of the planning, producing, and working.

Make boring to-dos fun. It's a lot more fun to get boring jobs, like dusting and lawn mowing, done when you're working together toward a common goal. Just make a challenge or a game out of it, and it turns it from boring to bonding.

Make sure the project appeals to everyone. Sure, painting your office soft lavender sounds fun to you, but if it doesn't appeal to your teenage son, then it's not going to help you to connect as a family.

Teen Challenges

If your teen is reluctant to pitch in, find something that is their specialty or an aspect of the project to let them participate in.

One of the biggest projects our family pulled off was before we were a family—our wedding. It was held in a friend's backyard and was a really homemade affair.

With getting married and blending a family with four teens, there was a lot of stress and reluctance over the whole event. So the kids were given jobs they would excel at. Jeremy helped pull together the music for the reception, and all the kids got to pick a song or two. This was the ultimate act of love and trust. We had the weirdest mix of wedding reception music you've ever heard. Our songs ranged from "I Can Only Imagine" by Mercy Me to "We Built this City on Rock 'n' Roll" by Jefferson Starship and "So Long and Thanks for All the Fish" from the movie *The Hitchhiker's Guide to the Galaxy*.

Kim and her best friend, Haley, were in charge of the guest quilt, a quilt my mom made and all our guests signed, and Justen was in charge of the soda and coffee bar. Everyone had a role, and it made it a day to remember, not just as a couple but also as a family.

Step It Up

Make sure that your activity is a comparison-free zone. In any project there's an opportunity for each person to shine. Be sure to call out what each person's contribution was and how it made a difference.

Suggestions for Singles

If the idea of getting a project up and running feels overwhelming, why not join something that is already happening at church or in your community? This gives your child an opportunity to make other adult connections and allows you to connect as well.

Connecting with Each Personality

Expressive

Hand over the aspects of the project that involve publicity or decor to your expressive child. If brightly colored markers or paint can be involved, all the better! She will happily paint the garage sale sign and stand on the street corner waving it at every car that drives by.

Analytical

Dealing with details is right up your analytical child's alley. Give him the parts of the project that involve listing, sorting, labeling, packing, and alphabetizing. He'll get them done to perfection.

Driving

Any parts of the project that can be quickly accomplished without a lot of time spent on minutiae can be delegated to your driving child. Keep her busy with clear, quick-to-finish tasks so she stays on her part of the project and doesn't try to jump ship to the supervision team.

Amiable

Your amiable child can become paralyzed by a large, seemingly overwhelming project. Break the big project into bite-sized chunks and hand them over one piece at a time.

Connection
6

Serving Together

Try This

Plan a time to serve together one-on-one with your child or as a family. It can be as small as helping a neighbor or as big as a mission trip.

Making the Connection

When was the last time you took time out of your busy family schedule to serve someone else?

One of our friends, Tammy, was feeling completely overwhelmed. She had just had her third child, and she felt as though life was getting away from her. She confessed at our weekly Bible study that her house was a wreck. She felt so underwater that she didn't know where to start.

After hearing what Tammy was going through, I could more than sympathize. I wanted to help. I had felt similarly overwhelmed when my colicky daughter, Kimberly, arrived on the scene. The only place she was happy was in my arms, and that didn't sit well with my toddler Justen or the state of our tiny apartment. I remember the feelings of wishing I could go back to bed or that someone, somewhere would just give me a break.

So as a family, we showed up on Tammy's doorstep, buckets and sponges in hand. We cleaned bathrooms, scrubbed floors, and cleaned off countertops. While Martha Stewart would not have been impressed with our efforts, Tammy was. It's amazing the difference a clean toilet can make when you're feeling like you can't deal with life.

But as much as it was a small gift to Tammy, it was also a small gift for me. My kids were not known to "whistle while they work" at home. As a matter of fact, grumbles could often be heard. But when they were helping at Tammy's house, they were all smiles. We were working as a team and having a great time doing it. Plus, there were a lot of teachable moments in the weeks after our impromptu Merry Maid brigade. We had discussions about serving, God asking us to care for our neighbors, as well as the value of our family's teamwork.

Is there a way for your family to serve together? Is there a family in need of help? A grandparent who could use some help around the house? A project at church that your family could work on together? Think through some different ideas and see what works for you.

When I think about serving together as a family, my thoughts turn to mission trips and building churches together in Mexico. I have several friends who have done those whole-family adventures and are the closer for it. But don't ignore the smaller serving opportunities right in your own backyard.

Make Connecting Fun

Service ideas for when your kids are preschoolers:

- Make colorful cards and deliver them to people in nursing homes.
- Invite a neighbor to play while his or her mommy goes grocery shopping kid-free.
- Serve family members. Together, wash Daddy's clothes or pick up big sister's toys.
- Rake leaves or pull weeds on your church's campus.
- Go through your toys and donate some to kids in need.

Service ideas for when your kids are grade-schoolers:

- Plant a community garden in your neighborhood.
- Pick up litter in a park.

- Start a neighborhood softball league or cycling group.
- Collect cans of food or coats for the needy.
- Deliver homemade muffins to your church office.
- Walk someone's dog.

Service ideas for when your kids are middle- and high-schoolers:

- Volunteer to help an older couple learn to use Skype so they can video chat with their grandkids.
- Write letters for servicemen and women.
- Help serve food in a local food kitchen.
- Record yourself reading a book and give the CD or wav.file (along with a copy of the book) to a day care center or a family with young kids.
- Mow someone's yard or shovel their driveway.
- Offer to watch someone's young kids while they take a much-needed day off.
- Bake a casserole for a busy family.
- Volunteer in the nursery or children's church.

Make Connecting Work

Here are my tips on making sure your family service project works.

Make your project age-appropriate. As great as it is to send care packages to soldiers in Iraq, if your kids are unable to comprehend the meaning of what you're doing, then the project is going to be just another chore for them. Instead, choose projects that will not only help the people you're serving, but will also allow your kids to understand how their sacrifice is making a difference.

Go short term. As fantastic as a two-week family mission trip to Honduras would be, serving in small ways can have a huge impact too. So even if you have only a free hour during the week, use that hour to serve someone in some way.

Do random acts of kindness. Model a willingness to serve every day by doing small acts of kindness for the people you encounter. Open a door for someone holding a baby. Anonymously pay for someone else's coffee. Offer to entertain a friend's squirmy toddler while she runs to the bank. Make serving others a part of your daily life—and your kids will catch on.

Serve your kids. Trust me, I get it. You already feel like your kids' personal servant, chef, and chauffeur. But make it a point to occasionally surprise your kids by doing a small act of service. Clean their room *for* them. Make a favorite meal. Pick up a copy of a just-released CD that you know your kid will love.

Teen Challenges

Find out what your teen is passionate about and see if there is a way to start serving in that area. It's important not to tell your teens to go serve because that's what they should do, but to model serving as a way of life.

Step It Up

My husband, Roger, and my daughter, Kimberly, have always had a different kind of relationship. Kimberly recently defined their relationship beautifully: "Yeah, we give each other a hard time, but if anyone else says anything against either of us, we'll gang up on them." As stepfather/stepdaughter relationships go, that's about the best thing I could've hoped for.

The fastest way that Roger and Kimberly bonded (besides a mutual love for teasing me about my coffee and Jane Austin addictions) is that they both love to work as techs in theater. Kimber was the tech director at her high school from her sophomore year on, and at various times Roger has been the worship arts director, tech director, or lighting director at the churches where he has served.

So when Roger had an opportunity to produce the Christmas musical at our church, he asked Kimber if she would like to help out as the stage manager. Kim was thrilled that she was given such a big role. Not only did Kim get the chance to serve, she got the chance to work with and serve alongside her stepdad.

Suggestions for Singles

When I was single, it was easy for me to feel alone and discouraged. I was working for a nonprofit at the time, and at various times, not only did my daughter volunteer with me, but so did Amanda, my future stepdaughter. It was great to be able to focus on serving, and while bonding with my daughter, also know we were helping people who needed us. It took the spotlight off my own issues, and God brought healing to me through the serving.

Connecting with Each Personality

Expressive

Your expressive child may initially balk at the idea of sharing your attention with someone else. Use her desire to feel special to help her empathize with those you will be serving. As she realizes "they're just like me," she's likely to join in with enthusiasm.

Analytical

Naturally perceptive, your analytical child has already noticed neighbors, church members, and even complete strangers in need. Ask him for suggestions and listen to his keen observations about who could benefit from a kind deed.

Driving

More task-oriented than relationship-focused, your driving child may initially hesitate at the idea of meeting people's needs. Once you reassure her that she'll be responsible for her own action, not other people's emotions, she'll be ready to help, full speed ahead!

Amiable

One of your amiable child's greatest gifts is *presence*. When invited, he'll sit for hours with a lonely senior, soothe a colicky baby, flea comb a cat, and do chores for others that you've never seen him lift a finger for at home.

Invest in Their Passion

Try This

Figure out what your child is passionate about and find a way to invest in it.

Making the Connection

What makes your kids giddy with excitement? An amazing song? Beautiful artwork? A last-minute home run with the bases loaded to win the game? An amazing bowl of salsa? Whatever it is that your kids are passionate about, I think one of the most powerful things you can do to connect with your kids is to invest in what they invest in.

My oldest, Justen, has always loved to write stories, and at a young age showed great ability as a storyteller. His characters were rich with detail, and his scenes were fun and fast-paced. So when he turned fifteen, we started to plan an adventure: Six days driving up through California and beyond until we hit the Oregon Shakespeare Festival in Ashland. And what determined our route? We spent a lot of time locating the best used bookstores (and bookstores that carried new books but also had a great used-books section) along the way.

We started with a night at my mom's house and took a detour based on her recommendation to visit the Almost Perfect Bookstore in Roseville, California. It was officially the first stop on our literary adventure. And after about a half hour in the store, I was concerned that it might be our last. I was afraid all the spending money Justen had saved over the past few months was going to be spent in one spot. His favorite author, Jim Butcher, had recently signed a few copies of his latest book for the store, and Justen wanted one. Bad.

Plop went his money (and maybe some of his grandmother's money that she had slipped to him without my knowledge), and Justen was in proud possession of a signed copy of his favorite author's latest release.

As far as Justen was concerned, the trip could have ended then.

But we soldiered on. We drove and listened to various audiobooks by Bill Bryson and to Donald Miller's *Blue Like Jazz*, we drank copious amounts of coffee, and we talked. We talked about life, we talked about writing, and we talked about God.

It ended up being one of the best memories I have with my son—and I learned so much about who he is, what he loves, and what he wants out of life. Of all my kids, Justen is the one I have to work the hardest at connecting with. And investing in his passions is the activity that has given me the biggest payoff.

We do the same thing when we're dating. Your boyfriend's into the Denver Broncos, so suddenly you're wearing orange and blue. She loves Japanese food, so you just bought a "Make Your Own Sushi" kit on Amazon. We do it because people love it when we want to hang out where they hang out. It makes them feel valued and special. It gives them a common language to speak with us. It changes the way they act and interact.

It's no different with our kids. When we get passionate about what they are passionate about, it changes our relationship.

Make Connecting Fun

Here are a few ideas on how to invest in your kids' passions.

If your child is passionate about music:

- Pull up her favorite artists on YouTube and listen to their songs.
- Take her to local coffee shops when they have live music and discuss what you like about the performance.

- Surprise her with concert tickets.
- Look up her favorite artists on Amazon and then download a new album from the "people who bought this, also bought…" section.
- Make it a standing date to watch *American Idol* or *The Voice* or whatever music show she's raving about.

If your child is passionate about sports:

- Play catch (or shoot hoops) with your kid, even if you can't throw a ball to save your life.
- Watch a game on TV with your kid and talk about his favorite players.
- Surprise him with tickets to a game (even the bleacher seats can be a ton of fun when you're watching together).
- Go to as many of his games or meets as possible and cheer him on from the sidelines.
- Look up articles about his favorite players, print them out, and put them on his bed.
- Order him a subscription to a sports magazine.
- See if any of your friends were once good at the sport your child loves and ask if they can mentor him.
- Sign up for a just-for-fun league and play together.

If your child is passionate about art:

- Become regulars at gallery openings and art museums in your town.
- Find prints online and order them to help decorate her room.
- Put a desk in your garage (or somewhere else that you're not worried about paint splatters) and make it her studio where she can paint, draw, and sculpt without worrying about the mess.

- Take an art class together.
- Go on a date to a paint-your-own-pottery shop.
- Volunteer to organize an art show at her school.

If your child is passionate about drama:

- Sign up your child for a local kids' theater troupe or club.
- Participate in your church's next musical or production... together.
- Watch movies together and discuss the acting instead of the plot.
- Get tickets to a play at a local small theater.
- Help your child practice reading scripts in front of the mirror.

If your child is passionate about fashion or beauty:

- Put together a list of blogs on fashion and then check them regularly for ideas.
- Go to the mall (leave your wallets at home if you want) and find three outfits for each of you that you love. Discuss what you love about them.
- Head to a local department store and get made over in the cosmetics section.
- Pick up a sketchpad and some colored pencils and encourage her to draw the designs she's dreaming up.
- Tear out pages in fashion magazines that you both like and hang them in her bedroom.
- Book appointments for manicures/pedicures or haircuts together.

If your child is passionate about sci-fi:

- Record *Clone Wars* or *Star Trek* and watch it together.

- Surprise him with tickets to a sci-fi convention.
- Go to the bookstore or library and find books you can read together.
- Start a collection—memorabilia, comic books, books— and help him find new items to add to it.
- Get a sci-fi trivia game and play it together.

If your child is passionate about writing and literature:

- Encourage your kid to journal regularly. Or get a journal and write each other letters back and forth.
- Read stories she's written and ask questions without being critical.
- Take her on a book-reading and writing adventure (like I did with Justen).
- Join a book club and participate together.
- Go to the bookstore with the goal of discovering a new author that neither of you has ever read.
- Read the same books at the same time and discuss what's happening. (Bonus: if you have an eReader or iPad, most e-books come with a license for six devices that are all owned by you, so you can both read the same book at the same time without buying it twice.)

If your child is passionate about food:

- Help your kid to plan and prepare one meal a week for the family.
- Go to good restaurants and order meals to share.
- Plant a garden together, then practice cooking new recipes with the bounty.
- Help your child prepare a bunch of tapas, and then invite your kid's friends over to taste everything you make.

- Ask to take a tour of the kitchen next time you go to your favorite restaurant.
- Take a cooking class together at a local restaurant, kitchen store, or community college.
- Get a subscription to a food magazine, and then select one or two recipes from each issue to make together.

If your child is passionate about travel:

- Check out travel guides from your library and read them together.
- Plan your dream vacation together. Even if you know you'll never be able to afford to make it a reality, it'll be fun to talk about together.
- Go on mini day-cations together. Head to local tourist attractions or just take a two-hour road trip into the country to have a picnic.
- Google some exotic locales and virtually visit those places from the comfort of your couch.
- Record travel shows (hello, Rick Steves) and discuss which locations you'd like to visit most.
- Plan an Italian night and make Italian food. Or a Mexican night and learn how to salsa dance by watching an online tutorial.

Make Connecting Work

Investing in your child's passions takes time (that you may not have) and money (that may be in short supply), but it's so important. Here are some of my best tips on how to make it work.

Learning the lingo. I have an advantage that one of Justen's great passions is also one of my great passions: writing. But he's a fiction writer and I write nonfiction. Plus, Justen's stories are fantasies (private detectives set in the future) where my books lean a lot more toward the practical. It may not seem that different to some people, but to me it might as well be the difference between learning Japanese and French. So I needed to learn about the style that Justen loved. I learned about plot and structure and character and tropes. I watch some of the same shows he does (*Castle*, the BBC's *Sherlock*) so we can talk about the finer points of fiction.

Whatever your child loves, you need to learn the lingo. Go to Wikipedia.com to brush up on the terms your child is using. Or read your son's magazine and impress him with your knowledge of all things skateboarding. Watch your daughter's favorite musician play or learn the names of the characters in her favorite play.

Create a fund for their passion. Put aside a small amount of money each month (and let them contribute too) to pay for supplies, classes, books, tickets, and more that relate to your child's passion. Perhaps all the money you get for recycling can go into a special jug. Or are there extra chores your child can do around the house to earn money for the fund?

Put your money where their passion is. I'm a patron of the arts. Justen's art that is. We've bought writing books, pens, and the special notebooks he likes to write in. I don't believe in going broke to support your kids' latest interest (we'll leave that to the parents on *Toddlers and Tiaras*), but I want to know enough about each of my kids' passions so when a birthday or Christmas rolls around, I can find something that will support what they love. Ask your child to put together a wish list of things they would like. When you (or Grandma) are looking for a gift they will love, you have a sure thing if they've picked it out themselves.

Be obsessed with them. Justen and I have spent many a day hanging out in a coffee shop, side-by-side typing away at our works-in-progress. It's great to have someone to mumble to when I can't find a quote I'm desperate for, or when one of his characters is not behaving the way Justen originally saw him. Even if I weren't a writer, I would still find a way to go with him to the coffee shop. I can check Facebook, pay bills, or plan a month of menus just as well from our local café as I can from home.

Find your peeps. I may not be an expert on fiction writing, but I know someone who is. My friend Shelley Bates is a fiction author and all-around great girl. Both Justen and Kimberly enjoy a type of fiction called steampunk, which is all about running things with steam instead of electricity (think Will Smith's *Wild Wild West*). Shelley has several books in the steampunk genre and is willing to talk to my eager kids about all things steam for hours on end. She even took the three of us to a Victorian-style ball with a steampunk theme. Shelley brought us to her house and dressed Kimber up in one of her Victorian costumes. While I never would have come up with any of these activities, I had a great time watching my kids enjoy Shelley. We talk about our adventure often, and I love that my kids have in their lives a godly woman they love.

Show the love. My stepson, Jeremy, became passionate about running while he was in high school. (And let me just say, going to cheer on your child when they're running long distance is the ultimate act of love. You see them for all of two minutes of a two-hour meet.) When Jeremy had his best time ever, my husband got a picture of him crossing the finish line. In Photoshop, Roger wrote out Jeremy's name, his personal best time, and the date on the lower right-hand corner of the photo. Jeremy, by far our most low-key kid, busted out with a huge grin when he saw the photo. Even though I will never participate in Jeremy's passion (there is no way I could keep up), there is tangible proof in our living room that we are invested in Jer.

Teen Challenges

I have a warning for you: The payoff doesn't always seem to be there, especially with teens. Many times I've sat in a café across from Justen with nothing more than an occasional grunt from the other side of the table. I'm not always sure he's even paying attention. But in the long run, my efforts to connect have shown him that his passions are important to me.

Step It Up

For years I was frustrated by my attempts to connect with Jeremy when it came to his passion for hockey. It was frustrating to sit through one of his games, only to have him ignore me afterward. All I had to show at the end of the game were blue fingers and the smelliest uniform in the world to wash. My showing up felt like a huge waste of time. But now that Jeremy is a young man, we can talk and laugh and reminisce about the hockey glory days. The payoff was long-term, not short-term. Your stepkids are going to be in your life for decades. It's important to invest in them now, while you're part of their everyday life, so that when they get older, they remember you were there.

Suggestions for Singles

When I was a single parent, my time, money, and energy were at an all-time low. It's doubly important to make sure that whatever effort and money you spend are directed as best they can be.

Why not sit down with your child and let them know what funds and times you have available, and then ask them to brainstorm with you about how to use both. Maybe it's taking a class together, signing up for some lessons, or simply hanging out together to talk about your kid's passion.

Connecting with Each Personality

Expressive

Your expressive child bores easily and thus can seem fickle with her passions. She'll likely flit from one new interest to the next within weeks, days, even hours. Just dive on in with her. She'll be thrilled that you're doing this together, and you won't have to go too deep.

Analytical

With your analytical child, you're in for in-depth research. He either knows, or wants to know, everything there is to know about his area of interest, down to the last exact term. Get ready to listen and learn all about their area of interest.

Driving

Take your vitamins and get your sleep; trying to keep up with a driving child can require the endurance of an iron-man trainee! In all seriousness, *ask* your child which activities she wants the two of you to do together, and trust her to be frank with you.

Amiable

One of the greatest gifts you can give your amiable child is simply your presence. You may find yourself sitting in a stadium watching him throw a pass or sitting on the floor of his room helping sort Legos. Just be there for him.

Connection
8

Brag on Your Kids…
According to Their Personality

Try This

Tell someone else how great your kid is in a way that best suits his or her individual personality.

Making the Connection

Remember how I told you in the last chapter that Justen is an excellent writer? Well, he is. He's great. I love reading his stories. I beam with pride every time he finishes a story, and I have to stifle the impulse to call my friend at the bookstore and warn her that a bestseller is on the way. He's *that* good.

I could go on and on about how great he is…but I just can't tell him. Why? Because he hates it.

A few weeks ago, I said to him, "I love what a creative writer you are!"

He looked at me like I was crazy and said, "I don't even know why you're telling me this." As if it were causing him grief to have to spend the energy listening to me.

Justen is an analytic/amiable personality. He's thoughtful and adaptable and nurturing…but he's also very pensive and private and slightly mortified to hear his mom go on and on about his work. So I've learned that a well-timed "nice job on that" says a lot more than hours of gushing.

My gushing was well-intentioned—I was proud of him and he really is a great writer. But my delivery? Well-intentioned or not, it didn't work. So instead of beaming with pride at my words, he scoffed. I now know that for him, less is more. Timing is everything. And my gushing on and on only makes me seem insincere.

I want you to brag on your kids in a way that really makes them proud of their accomplishments—and in a way that's best received by their individual personality type. So for this challenge, I want you to brag on your child in a way that makes them feel loved, appreciated, and proud.

Make Connecting Fun

It's one thing to brag about your kids. It's an entirely different thing to brag about them in the way they best understand affirmation—in their personal brag language, if you will. Cheri Gregory explains exactly how to do that for each personality type:

If your kid is an Expressive child:

- Gush, gush, gush! It's all about them, and they could hear it all day!

- Use super superlatives. They're the best thing *ever* to an expressive child.

- Sincerity is optional (just kidding…mostly).

- Bragging in front of their friends is fabulous. Just make sure you go on and on (and on).

- Let your kid linger in the limelight.

If your kid is an Analytical child:

- Remember this child's mantra: Publicity = attention = death.

- Remember their mantra number two: Gushing = insincerity = worse than nothing.

- Try writing a heartfelt letter or an e-mail that notices the details.

If your kid is a Driving child:

- Keep it short and bottom line: what did they do and what was the impact?

- Focus on what they *did,* not on bragging about or praising them as a person.

- Publicly is OK if it's quick and especially if important people witness it. Bragging *to* the important people within this child's hearing is especially good strategy!

If your kid is an Amiable child:

- Bragging on them in private is best. If you brag about them in front of others, they'll worry that it will make the others feel bad.

- If they feel known and understood, "Great job!" or "Thank you!" says everything.

- The more you go into details, the more they may feel you're bluffing and making stuff up as you go along.

- Affirmation from someone they respect, such as a pastor or a teacher, carries tremendous weight.

Make Connecting Work

Your kids are pretty great, aren't they? Bragging about them is easy. The hard part is knowing how to draw the line between being *that* mom (you know, the one who's constantly rattling on and on about how her six-year-old has already been accepted into an Ivy League school) and being someone who is truly proud of her kids. Here are a few tips to make bragging about your kids work:

- Brag about their effort instead of their accomplishments: "Wow, you worked really hard on that project!"

- Do it in front of your kid. There's no use talking about them if they're not there to soak up the glory.

- Make it infrequent enough not to be annoying. Your kid does great things all the time. But truthfully, no one except for Grandma wants to hear that your kid got an A on his daily spelling test for the fifty-fourth day in a row. So when you're bragging to other people—and you should from time to time—make sure it's about something big enough to really matter to your kid.

- Keep a brag journal in your purse. Whenever your kid does something great—such as holding a door for a stranger or saying thank you without being prompted— jot it down and then read your list together at bedtime.

- Share with everyone at the dinner table a few things your kid did really well that day (that is, if your kid is an expressive or a driving child and likes people to hear about their accomplishments).

Teen Challenges

I've found that the best way to brag on my teens is to tell a loose-lipped relative. If I brag on them to their grandma, she is sure to tell my kids, "Your mom tells me…" It means more knowing that I'm spreading good gossip about them.

Step It Up

Want to blow your stepkids' minds? Go out of your way to brag on them to your spouse. Make a big deal about how much they helped you to get dinner on the table or that you noticed them showing kindness to a sibling.

Suggestions for Singles

As hard as it is sometimes for me to deal with my ex, I need to remember that the most important role he plays in my life is not as my ex but as the parent of my children. I try to point out every chance I get, all the great stuff my kids got from their dad. "You are so brilliant with numbers, just like your father!" or "You have a heart for serving others. I've seen that so often in your dad, and now I see it in you!"

Connection
9

Build a Legacy

Try This

Map out your family's legacy.

Making the Connection

A few years ago, I overheard Kimberly trying to make plans to work on a school project with a friend. Her friend suggested Sunday night, and Kimber immediately said, "Oh, I can't. We have family night on Sundays."

Even now, we still have family night on Sunday nights. And our kids—who are all grown and living on their own—still keep their schedules free and join us for dinner, games, and time to talk. It's just something our family does.

Whenever your kid says, "Well, that's just something my family does," he or she is identifying themselves with your family unit and everything your family stands for. By building family traditions, establishing family values, and giving voice to your family's missions, you're building a legacy for your kid.

For this connection, I want you to sit down with your kids and talk about what your family just *does*, whether it's Saturday morning pancakes or yearly mission trips to Uganda. Then make a list and post it somewhere your family can see it and refer to it every day.

Make Connecting Fun

On my desk, I have a tiny framed verse: "Pray continually"—1 Thessalonians 5:17. This little framed verse is the cornerstone of our family legacy. And surrounding that verse is the frame, which reminds me of the other five tenets of our family legacy:

Faithfulness

Responsibility

Attitude

Mercy

Encouragement

Here's my family's legacy list to help inspire you:

1. In our family, we pray for each other.

In his book *Prayer: Does It Make Any Difference?*, Philip Yancey notes, "Most of my struggles in the Christian life circle around the same two themes: why God doesn't act the way we want God to, and why I don't act the way God wants me to." He goes on to say, "Prayer is the precise point where those themes converge."

I've struggled to make it a priority to make my house a house of prayer. And I've made my best effort to model prayerfulness to my children from the time they were little kids. I pray (both aloud and on my own) for each of my children to grow in the attributes God wants to see in them. I pray as they wrestle with challenges. I pray as they make decisions. And I daily pray and thank God for each family member.

I've also worked to create an environment where sharing prayer requests is a natural part of being in our family. I let my kids know that when they are struggling with a decision, not only am I there to talk about it, but I'm praying about it, whether they want to talk or not.

Prayer is our most important family legacy. But we have five other principles we value as well.

2. In our family, we value faithfulness.

"All you need to say is simply 'Yes' or 'No'; anything beyond this comes from the evil one" (Matthew 5:37).

My Kimberly is a smart cookie. When she was about three, her pediatrician said to me, "Either that kid is going to get into a world of hurt, or she is going to be the leader of a small nation. Good luck with that." Gulp.

One of Kim's nicknames was "The Negotiator." She was forever bargaining, reasoning, and lawyering to try to extend bedtimes, stay home from school on days that didn't sound interesting to her, not eat zucchini, and avoid other things that I deemed she needed to do.

And sometimes, I would give in. It's exhausting "discussing" things with a five-year-old the whole way home from school, every single day. But I noticed that every time I relented and gave in to one of her demands (thinking, *Just this one time…*), she would use it against me in future arguments.

Oh yeah. She was that good.

When you have a child who is unrelenting, it is doubly important to not compromise. When your yes is yes, and your no is no, you are demonstrating faithfulness. If you say you are going to be home in five minutes and you haven't been through the checkout line, it's time to call your kids and give them a more accurate estimate of your arrival time. We would want them to do the same for us if they were running late.

I know for many of us, our initial reaction is, "But I'm the parent. I don't have to answer to my child." You're right. But this isn't answering to your child, it's letting them know when you say something, you mean it. Your word is faithful. Your actions are faithful. There are few things sadder than a kid who doesn't believe their parent.

Let your kids know that you mean what you say, and they should as well. We want our kids to grow up with this trait so that when they are married or working or a part of a church community, everyone will see their faithfulness.

3. In our family, we're responsible.

It's simple—if you have a chore, you do a chore. You are responsible for your own actions and the consequences. Yes, there is grace. Your freedom grows in our family not because of your age but because of the responsibility you have shown.

4. In our family, we have a good attitude.

We can rise above "that's just how I am" thinking.

> You were taught, with regard to your former way of life, to put off your old self, which is being corrupted by its deceitful desires; to be made new in the attitude of your minds; and to put on the new self, created to be like God in true righteousness and holiness (Ephesians 4:22-24).

Our kids can recognize real change in our lives when we are honest and transparent with them about how God is changing us.

5. In our family, we lead with mercy.

We can trust each other to do what's in the other person's best interests. We don't gossip about each other. We always forgive. We help each other out. We apologize when we're wrong.

> Speak and act as those who are going to be judged by the law that gives freedom, because judgment without mercy will be shown to anyone who has not been merciful. Mercy triumphs over judgment. (James 2:12-13).

It doesn't matter how "right" we are. If we don't lead with love and mercy, we are not living as God wants us to.

6. In our family, we encourage others to be what God created them to be.

Our kids have their own thoughts, opinions, and ideals. They are encouraged to share those, respectfully, with the rest of the family.

My kids' careers, families, and relationships with God are going to look different than mine. Sometimes that's hard, but I also don't want my kids to have a hand-me-down faith, or feel that because they have different ideas of how to express themselves, they will not be celebrated. We encourage our kids to be exactly who God designed them to be.

Make Connecting Work

We all leave a legacy to our kids—intended or not. So how can we make sure the legacy we leave helps them to become the people God wants them to become?

Make your legacy not only about what you are, but also about what you aren't. A family in our church goes on a yearly two-week mission trip. I think that's so cool. Many times I've thought, *Oh, we should do something like that.* But the truth is, as we've prayed about the opportunities, God has never said yes. He's said yes to supporting missionaries and hosting them in our home, but we have other ministries.

I went on the mission field several times as a single, and I think foreign missions are really important, but it's just not part of our family legacy. However, serving in our community, that is us. Serving at church, writing books, speaking to teen-mom groups, supporting kids overseas, that is part of our family legacy.

You can learn from your kids just as much as they can learn from you. I think you'll agree that raising kids is a learning experience. And I've found that I often learn more from my kids than they learn from me. So look at your family legacy as a way that each member in the family can not only learn and grow, but also teach others.

A family legacy is not a set of rules. It's easy to let a family legacy boil down to a set of rules—let your kid stick a sticker on a chart every time she's kind and call it good. But a family legacy is actually a point of identity for your kids. So instead of looking at it like a list of "should dos" or "oughta dos," help them to see it as just the way you *are.* This is us. This is who God made us to be. And this is who God wants us to be.

Teen Challenges

For some teens, it's going to feel like you're changing the rules midway through their life if you come at them with a set of ideals. Don't lay down a new set of laws; just change the way that you talk about the characteristics of your family—what you want to live up to as a godly family.

Step It Up

When Roger and I started talking with our kids about our family legacy, we got a lot of resistance. Some at first really resisted the word *family*. But when we said, "In our home, we encourage each other. In our home, we talk to each other with respect." The change of one word (*family* to *home*) made all the difference.

Suggestions for Singles

Single parents, make your kids a partner in creating your family ideals. What does your child want to see come out of your legacy? Brainstorm some ideas and see what feels right for your family as a team.

Connecting with Each Personality

Expressive

Because your expressive child wants to be popular, he may eagerly participate in family legacies. That is, until there are social repercussions. When friends tell him that his family is "just plain weird," your dialogues of support will become yet another family legacy.

Analytical

Your analytical child loves knowing and following "the rules," and carrying on your family's legacy is a job they are well suited for. You'll need to help your child realize that rules don't supersede relationships; family members who do not honor the family legacies are still welcomed, loved, and respected.

Driving

Your driving child may regularly test the boundaries you've set. When it comes to family legacy issues, be ready to demonstrate that they are still in place and holding strong. Spoken in love, the statement "When you're in your own place, you can choose...but in this home *we*..." can offer an immature driving child immense security.

Amiable

Your amiable child tends to comply with the expectations of those she's with, just to keep the peace. You can help her practice standing loyal to family values in situations where the easiest—and least conspicuous—option is to conform to "what everyone else is doing."

Get the Conversation Started

Try This

Have a meaningful conversation at the table.

Making the Connection

Have you ever had a dinnertime conversation that sounded like this?

You: "How was your day?"

Your kid: "Fine."

You: "OK, so, what did you do at school?"

Your kid: Unintelligible grunts followed by a harried shoveling of food.

You: "Soooooo, who did you hang out with?"

Your kid: "Moooo-om."

Conversation over and out.

We've all been there. Conflict. Stress. Just plain exhaustion. Whatever the cause, sometimes even our most well-intentioned family times unravel into silence as the entire family quickly finishes their food and asks to be excused.

We already talked in Connection 2 about the importance of having family dinner, but there's more to family dinner than just eating together. There isn't much connecting going on when dinnertime is a chorus of grunts, eye rolls, and "moooo-*oms.*"

But here's the thing: when your family is eating, you have an (almost) captive audience. Your kids have to eat. And while they're shoveling in your chicken parm, they (I hope) don't have toys or home-work or TV in front of them. So it's the perfect time to start purpose-ful conversations with your kids. And that's what I'm challenging you to do today.

Make Connecting Fun

Here are a few ideas on how to get talking at the table.

Ask questions that require more than a one-word answer. I find myself doing it a lot: "How was your day?" "How was your math test?" "Who did you hang out with?" Instead, try questions that require longer answers. "What was the best thing that happened to you today?" or "What part of the math test was most challenging?" or "Tell me one funny thing that your friend Suzi said today."

Go beyond dinner. By the end of the day, your kids (and you) are probably tired and ready for some R & R. So, maybe dinner isn't always the best time for deep and meaningful conversations. Try start-ing a deep conversation over pancakes on Saturday morning. Or set-ting up a fancy-schmancy afternoon tea with cups, saucers, and little tiny scones.

To be continued. Not every conversation has to be wrapped up with a little bow and finished in an hour. Instead, say something like, "Hey, it's time to get ready for bed right now, but I'm really enjoying this con-versation. Can we continue it tomorrow at dinner?"

Be intentional with little ones. Preschoolers are a tough set. They're easily distracted. They don't necessarily connect on a deep level. And their idea of intriguing often involves a pee-pee joke and a silly song. But with some intentional finesse, you can have deep conversations even with them. Just think of yourself as a director who has to con-stantly steer the conversation in the direction you want it to go.

Get thematic. I remember a night that I made a taco bar and then used it as a starting place to talk about our "kid honeymoon." When Roger and I got married, he and I took a honeymoon, and then a few weeks later, all six of us went on a three-day cruise that started in Long Beach and made a stop in Ensenada. With our Mexican-themed meal, we had a blast reminiscing about our adventures as we took a "cultural tour" and all the street vendors assumed that Kimberly was an easy mark and would follow her down the streets hawking their wares.

Make Connecting Work

Of course—as those of you with teenagers are well aware—conversation doesn't just naturally flow. It takes intentional effort and some knowledge of the right things to say to get the conversation moving. Here are a few conversation starters from the book *150 Quick Questions to Get Your Kids Talking* by my friend Mary DeMuth:

10 Discussion Starters to Get Your Family Chatting

1. What is the bravest thing you've ever done?

2. Describe the ideal spouse. (Parents, how would you have answered this question before you met your spouse?)

3. Describe a time when you were jealous of a friend. What happened? Why were you jealous?

4. What was the best thing that happened to you when you were five? (Change the age if another one works better.) The worst?

5. What toy did you want that you never received? Do you still want it now?

6. If you could be amazing at any sport, what would it be and why?

7. If you could write a letter to anyone in the world and were guaranteed he or she would write back, who would you write? What would you write?

8. How would your best friend describe you?

9. If you were to design housing for the homeless in your city or town, what would you include? A restaurant? A gym?

10. Who is the funniest person you know? Why is he or she funny?

Teen Challenges

You may think that your teens won't want to do something as dumb as respond to questions at the dinner table. Think again. Cheri Gregory came up with this list of "Teen Appropriate" questions. Both Cheri's and my kids still love to share their opinions and ideas—if the questions are compelling enough.

Would you give up junk food if it meant you'd live ten years longer?

What's your favorite summertime activity?

Would you rather fly or be invisible?

Which of your ancestors would you most like to meet?

Which TV show would you pick to live inside for a week?

What are the most important qualities you look for in a friend?

When are old things better than new things?

What's the best birthday celebration you can imagine?

If you could master one instrument, what would you choose?

What three things would you like to change in the world?

Would you rather be a great musician, athlete, scientist, artist, politician, or writer?

How does a person become courageous?

If you could have any view from your bedroom window, what would it be?

What's your favorite family tradition?

What personality trait has gotten you in the most trouble?

What's in your ultimate ice-cream sundae?

Where would you choose to travel if money were no object?

In order of importance, how would you rank happiness, money, freedom, and love?

What fear would you like to conquer?

Which animal would you love to be for a day?

Would you rather live for a week in the past or a week in the future?

What event in the past or future would you like to witness in person?

What's the scariest thing that ever happened to you?

What would you most like to ask God?

If you were showing a foreigner around your town, where would you take them?

What's your definition of integrity and do you have it?

What do you like best and least about your life?

How is your family different from other families and what are the pros and cons?

What would you save first if your house caught fire?

What's your proudest accomplishment?

What's the hardest thing you've ever done?

What wild animal would you love to tame and keep as a pet?

In what ways are you generous?

What do children know more about than adults?

What would you like to be doing in ten years?

What's a good loser and are you one?

What do you worry about the most?

What strengths do you bring to your family and do you feel they are appreciated?

Which of your five senses would you least want to give up?

If you had the time and resources, what kind of volunteer work would you like to do?

Who is one of your heroes and why do they inspire you?

Step It Up

Tread gently here. Let the biological parent start asking the questions first, and then mix it up. Kids may not want to participate because they think it's dumb. Questions don't have to be random. Ask them about their favorite band or their favorite toy to play with—anything they would naturally love to talk about.

Suggestions for Singles

If your children spend time with another family member (their other parent, their other grandparents), they may feel the need to clam up and not share those details in order to keep from hurting you. Make sure your kids know that the dinner table is a safe place to share. Look how single mom Jill made her dinner table a safe place.

> When I became a single mom, dinner time was the last thing I wanted to do. But I knew it was important for my kiddos. We came up with the idea of talking about Highs and Hopes at dinner. We take turns with who goes first, and we share our high for the day (or if they've been at their dad's, their high during that time) and then our hope for the upcoming day. I have learned lots about the other part of my kids' life and enjoy connecting and being able to support their hopes.

Connecting with Each Personality

Expressive

Your chatterbox expressive child can act as if he believes that God placed him on earth to fill every silence with talking. Ask him to think of a secret signal you can give that means "It's time to be quiet and count to 100" so others can participate in the conversation.

Analytical

Honesty is a vital virtue for your analytical child. So she may believe in telling the truth. The *whole* truth. And nothing but the entire, elaborate, detailed truth. The fact that not everyone values every single fact the way she does will likely shock and deeply sadden her, but you'll have to break the news to her. Often.

Driving

Short. To the point. Bottom line. This is the kind of communication your driving child values, so this is what he typically gives and expects to get. You may have to help him develop the patience to not interrupt stories that "go on and on and on" (i.e., last longer than fifteen seconds).

Amiable

Because your ever-fair amiable child wants to see all sides to an issue, she needs time to mull over a question, ponder the various implications, and eventually come up with an answer. Be aware that a question asked tonight may produce an answer tomorrow...next week...next Christmas. And it'll be well worth the wait!

Connection
11

Go Outside

Try This

Spend some time in the great outdoors with your kids.

Making the Connection

I'm not what you would call an "outdoor girl." I hate camping. Once when my kids were little, we went with my in-laws on a camping trip. They were so excited because they had just bought a new camper and wanted to give it a spin. As I heard them list all the amenities of their new rig, I thought to myself, *This kind of camping doesn't seem so bad.*

They had several beds in the camper, a full if tiny kitchen, and a toilet. OK, this is how camping should be. We were going to be camping like human beings and not like the people on Survivor.

It wasn't until we got there that I found out the truth. They'd all tricked me. That comfy mattress to snuggle up on? The camper slept only four—my in-laws and my kids. My husband and I had to pitch a tent next to the luxury camper.

Oh, and that fully stocked kitchen? No one told me that one of the cardinal rules of camping is that as soon as you're done cleaning up from one meal, it's time to start cooking the next. And there wasn't room to wash dishes inside the camper, so I was relegated to a bucket and a hose behind the camper. (Apparently an unwritten rule of camping is that everything related to food is work for the womenfolk.)

And the toilet? That was for use only in the middle of the night—you know, for the people sleeping *in* the camper. Those of us relegated to the tent had to take a midnight hike with flashlight to the deluxe accommodations (there were two holes in the plank to sit on).

I was trying (maybe not too hard) to buck up and be a good camper. That is, until it started to rain.

And rain.

And rain some more.

It was a cross between a horror movie (don't go into the outhouse alone) and the dumbest slapstick comedy (as I fall face-first into the mud) you've ever seen.

Did I mention I'm not a fan of the outdoors?

So when Roger and I were dating and he asked me if I liked camping, my answer was obvious. No. No, I don't like the taste of dirt in my food. No, I work really hard to earn money so I can live indoors. No, I don't like smelling like a combination of bug repellent and desperation. No.

But that's not what I said. I was falling in love with Roger, and I wanted him to fall in love with me. So I said yes. "Yes, I love camping. They call me Camping Kathi. Didn't you know?" (Don't judge. Before we got married, Roger *loved* to go shoe shopping with me.)

It's a mixed marriage, granted, but we've made it work. And for Roger's sake, and the sake of our kids, I've learned to tolerate the outdoors. And the fact that Roger bought me a reclining camping chair, a book light, and a Coleman coffeepot didn't hurt matters.

Now for Roger's birthday each year we go day camping. And I have to tell you, for the most part I look forward to it. It's truly a chance to literally unplug for the day. Where we go to day camp there is no cell or Internet reception. We are all forced to put down our cell phones, Kindles, and iPads and actually hang out together (after about 30 minutes of our kids holding their phones to the sky, unconvinced there is a place on earth that doesn't have wifi. Once they lose their will to live and give up on connecting, they actually put down their electronics and have a great time.)

Things are so different from when I was young. My mom would

send us outside to play with the other kids on our block, and we wouldn't come home until dinner was ready or the streetlights went on (or until my mom started yelling at the top of her lungs). Nowadays, we are much more aware of the dangers that lurk, and the only way for most kids to enjoy the outdoors is with a parent.

But time outside is so important. It gives your kids time to escape the noise and distractions of media, get some fresh air, get some exercise, and burn some energy. And even a not-so-outdoorsy girl like me can admit that nature reflects God's beauty in a way that nothing else can.

So what are you waiting for? Let's go outside.

Make Connecting Fun

When Justen and Kimberly were in elementary school, their dad and I took them to Butchart Gardens in Victoria, British Columbia. It was a place I had always wanted to visit. I love flowers and was excited to see this place that over a dozen people said we had to visit. Sadly, my kids did not share my enthusiasm. They had already decided that looking at flowers was going to be *boring* and were going into it with grumpy attitudes.

Their dad decided that instead of a standoff, he would turn the visit into a game. He told them if they found fifty of the flowers that were featured in the visitor's guide, he would give them each five Canadian dollars. (This made the prize even more intriguing, since it was foreign money and therefore very exotic.) My kids had a great day running from flower to flower, looking it up in their guidebooks, asking either me or their dad for help in tracking things down. They even wanted their pictures taken with their favorite (read *weirdest*) flowers. What could have been a miserable trip turned into an adventure my daughter still talks about.

30 Connecting Activities to Do Outside

1. Cook pancakes on your barbecue.

2. Go for a treasure hunt in your neighborhood. Here's a short list of things for your kids to find: a leaf bigger

than their hand, a rock smaller than their little toe, and something they can recycle.

3. Shop at a farmers' market (sampling is encouraged).

4. Tape butcher paper to your fence and create a painted mural.

5. Sleep outside.

6. Pop Jiffy Pop popcorn over an open fire.

7. Play cards outside (but not on a windy day).

8. Read a book on a quilt on your grass.

9. Use chalk to create sidewalk art.

10. Jump rope.

11. Set up a camping tent on your back lawn for a trial run before a camping trip.

12. Walk your dog or a neighbor's dog.

13. Build a pizza box solar oven (you'll find some great directions at www.solarcooker-at-cantinawest.com/pizza_box_solar_oven.html).

14. Do some lawn bowling. Save up ten soda bottles, milk cartons, macaroni-and-cheese boxes—whatever you can collect. Use a ball to knock them over.

15. Go fishing.

16. Take a picnic to the beach.

17. Hike.

18. Watch a sunset.

19. Watch a sunrise.

20. Build a birdfeeder out of a gourd.

21. Plant a butterfly garden.

22. Wash the car together.

23. Wash the dog together.

24. Find festivals in your area and plan a day to attend.

25. Make sun tea.

26. Have a father-daughter tea party (stuffed animals are invited).

27. Run through the sprinklers.

28. String lights in your trees.

29. Play soccer (bonus: a calf workout for you without a trip to the gym).

30. Build an obstacle course and navigate it together.

Make Connecting Work

Here are some simple ideas to help you make it a habit to spend some time, several times a week, outdoors with your kids:

Create Some Space

The lure of the TV, Internet, video games, and everything pluggable is too seducing for most kids, and if we're honest, for us as well. Create a time every day where you are in a "No Plug Zone." Maybe it's from three to six every afternoon where your home is free from e-distractions. When you create some space and don't have to tear your kids away from a show designed to hold their interest for thirty minutes, it will be much easier to get your family outside.

Make It Good for You

This is a parenting book, so I'm supposed to tell you all these fun activities your kids will love to do outside—and I will. But if your goal is to get outside with your kids as much as possible, you need to want to go outside. So I suggest concentrating on making it fun for you as well. Here are some ideas to get you out of doors that not only your kids will enjoy, but you will as well.

Get dressed. So your kids are wearing the latest from the L.L. Bean catalog, but you're making do with your college sweatshirt while keeping your hands tucked into your sleeves to ward off frostbite. If you want to connect with your kids outdoors, make sure you're comfortable outdoors. Get some good walking shoes as often as you need them, and treat yourself to a new bathing suit at least every half decade.

Explore the neighborhood. As much fun as it is to go to the beach or the mountains, see how you can incorporate being outdoors into your everyday routine. Go for a walk and find the best parks, trails, and attractions in your neighborhood. Even if you're heading for the indoors (the grocery store or the library), don't automatically jump in the minivan. You'll get in some exercise, plus you get bonus points if you go on a walk with your kids and get the ingredients for tomorrow's dinner all at the same time.

Pack it up. Make sure if you're bringing some drinks and snacks that you have something besides organic fishy crackers. Get some yummy trail mix that you eat only out of doors. You're burning off the calories, so go nuts (and dried fruit)!

Get equipped. If you don't own a bike, could you borrow one so that you and your kiddos can ride together? Or how about some day-camping equipment? That stuff goes for cheap at garage sales so don't buy new unless you have to. Plus, camping stuff is among the easiest to borrow since most people use their gear only a few times a year.

Spruce Up Your Outdoor Space

Whether you have a backyard, a patio, a terrace, or a fire escape, just a little thought (and maybe a birthday gift or two) will make it so much more fun for Mom and Dad to be outside.

Get a mom/dad chair. A few years ago on Mother's Day, Roger got me a chair and ottoman for our backyard. I love that chair. I do my devotions there during the warmer months, and I love hanging outdoors talking to the kids and my husband during the fall.

Hook up the iPod. Yes, there are times I like listening to the sounds of nature, but there are other times that I want Bono singing to me.

Make it pretty. Plant flowers and shade trees. Have a bird bath and hummingbird feeder positioned where you can see them. Treat your outdoor space as an extension of your home, and make it a place that's hard to resist.

Fire it up. A lot of the time spent in the backyard at our house is around fire: barbecuing as well as drinking hot cocoa around the outdoor fireplace are some of our favorite family times. There is just something about a fire that brings a family out of their daily routines and slows everyone down. Marshmallows (toasted or not) are a great addition to the cocoa.

Teen Challenges

If you can truly get away from it all (i.e., no wireless connection), you can experience a different child. I will admit that when it was at its worst, our kids had connection withdrawal from their phones that felt physically painful for them. But after an hour or so of climbing into the nearest tree to try to establish cell reception, they finally relaxed and made a connection with the rest of the family.

Step It Up

You can turn grudging outdoorsmen (and women) into a regular Bear Grylls by making an effort to connect outdoors in fun and creative ways. Just the fact that you are doing some normal activities in a not so normal way—outside—lets your stepkids drop some of their guard and connect in fresh ways. (This has even been tested on teenagers and proven to work 80 percent of the time in our home.)

Suggestions for Singles

If you are new to the great outdoors, admit it. Learn together with your kids and let them take the lead on some activities. While you must always play the role of the parent and not a partner, there is an opportunity for your child to develop skills and feel the accomplishment of teaching you how to do some of the things she learned in Girl Scouts about camping.

Connecting with Each Personality
Expressive

Encourage your expressive child to find the party element in your outdoor ventures. Camping becomes "one big slumber party for the entire family." A walk through the neighborhood becomes "a trash collection party." Playing Frisbee on the front lawn can even become "a sprinkler party"!

Analytical

Assign your analytical child the task of making the list of "necessary equipment" for your outdoor excursion. (Invite her shopping only if you plan to buy every single item on her list!) Then enlist her help packing and repacking. It's wonderful having at least one person along who knows exactly where everything is.

Driving

The primary issue for your driving child is what on earth he's supposed to *do* while on this family outdoor adventure. When you hand him a digital camera or camcorder and ask him to document the trip, you're giving him a much-needed sense of purpose.

Amiable

Your amiable child is in her natural habitat when she's out in nature. Allow her plenty of unscheduled time to look for wildflowers, look at all the birds, and listen to the wind whispering through tree branches, and she'll be one happy camper.

A Treat Just for Them

Try This

Pick up or make a special treat just for your kid.

Making the Connection

I'm all about fair. I keep track of how many gifts we get for each kid at Christmas. We have the same "meet you halfway when buying your first car" arrangement for each of the kids. We work really hard to keep things fair.

Until it comes to Christmas stockings. All of my kids are chocolate fiends except one. So Amanda, Jeremy, and Kimberly each get a chocolate orange (you know, the kind you whack on the table and it breaks into sections). Woe is me if they don't get one. One kid is known to feel the stocking every year to ensure there will be a chocolate orange.

My oldest, Justen, couldn't care less about chocolate. He wants Gummi Bears. So every year, each kid has identical stockings except Justen. And that's the way he likes it.

In most houses, treats are of the lowest-common-denominator variety. We'll get a cheese pizza because everyone likes something different. Most birthday cakes are plain vanilla or chocolate. But every once in a while it's great to indulge a child and get them their heart's desire. Which is why for this connection, I'm asking you to get a special treat for your kid—something that's special so your kid will know that you went out of your way to pick something just for them.

129

Make Connecting Fun

My stepdaughter, Amanda, *loves* my artichoke dip. So I make that for her each and every holiday. I even gave her the recipe so she could make it herself, but she says hers doesn't taste as good. That's about the best thing you can say to a mom or stepmom.

Anyway, think about a food your kid just loves. It doesn't have to be sweet—for some kids, the best treat you can get them is a bag of Doritos or a pepperoni pizza. Then connect with that child by picking up or making that item *just for them*. Here are some ideas:

Take your kid out. After Justen had one particularly grueling week at school, I picked him up from school and headed to one of our favorite ice-cream places. He had his plain chocolate and I had my low-fat rocky road. It spoiled his dinner (and mine), but it was totally worth it.

Introduce your kid to your favorite childhood treats. Did you just love Wonka Bottle Caps or those three-foot-long licorice ropes when you were a kid? Pick some up and introduce your kid to the candies you wax nostalgic about. (Can't find what you want? Head to www .candywarehouse.com where you can pick up nearly every kind of candy ever made.)

Bring them breakfast in bed. Load a tray with eggs and bacon or run out for a box of doughnuts and deliver it to your kid in bed along with a comic book and a glass of fresh-squeezed orange juice. And yes, go ahead and stay in their room to eat with them—just no fretting over crumbs in the sheets.

Give your kid something to come home to. Setting out freshly baked homemade cookies (yes, the kind from the refrigerator section totally count as homemade) and milk when your kid comes home from school is a great way to show them you were thinking about them when they were gone.

Be a short-order cook...just once. Picture this: A hot day, cold glasses of iced tea in hand, chips and Roger's famous salsa on the table, and steaks on the grill. Sounds like a perfect family dinner, right? It was. Except that Kimberly hates steak. So I decided to surprise her and do something special. While Roger grilled the steaks for everyone else, I whipped up a batch of her favorite pesto marinade and made her a pesto-grilled chicken breast. Sure, it took a bit of work, but she was ecstatic that I went out of my way to make her something she loved.

Drinks are treats too. On a particularly hot day, stop at a drive-in and pick up an icy lemonade. Pass it back to your kid and tell them they looked like they could use some refreshment.

Figure out how to make their favorite foods. Justen loves the Greek lemon soup we get at this little Greek joint down the road. So instead of spending a fortune every time he gets a craving, I've learned to make it and to surprise him with a pot from time to time.

Make Connecting Work

I actually have some rules for this connection. (I know, aren't I being bossy?)

Rule 1: The treat has to be just for your child. My reason? You probably give your kids foods they like or enjoy all the time. I mean, it's not like you serve boiled fish and mushy peas for dinner every night, do you? So for this connection, you have to pick up a treat that's just for them.

Rule 2: Make it special. This isn't one of those grab-a-few-cookies-in-the-cupboard-and-call-it-a-treat types of connections (not that there's anything wrong with cookies in the cupboard). For this connection, you have to make their treat something special. Something they don't get every day. Something that shouts "I love you and I want you to know it!"

Teen Challenges

I spent a lot of time hiding food from my teens. If we were having a birthday party on Saturday and I bought a case of Henry Weinhard's Root Beer for our celebration, I couldn't even dream of leaving those out in the open. Not if I wanted to make sure they were present and accounted for at the party. However, I could be a hero by letting one of the kids who was home alone with me have a "tester" root beer. It's the little things in life that make our kids happy.

Step It Up

Even before I became their stepmom, I knew that my stepkids (and their dad) loved Goofy's Cherry Sour Balls candy from Disneyland. Even if Roger ordered the candy, he would always give it to me so I was the one to give it to Amanda and Jeremy. Just another way to say "I love you and I'm thinking about you."

Suggestions for Singles

I know that money is tight, but just remember—buying each person (including you) a treat they love often has a bigger impact than buying a big treat that everyone likes. Instead of getting the giant tub of vanilla ice cream, treat each of you to your favorite ice cream in a smaller size.

Connecting with Each Personality

Expressive

Your expressive child loves surprises. The fact that you thought about her and went to all the trouble of getting something just for her (and nobody else) automatically makes it—regardless of what it may be—her new favorite treat in the whole wide world. And it makes you her new favorite person, at least for the next five minutes.

Analytical

Never guess when treating your analytical child. He knows exactly what he does and does not like, and he believes that anyone who truly loves him knows these details as well. Watch and listen for his favorite food, drink, and candy down to the brand and exact flavor. Don't try to fudge with "close enough." Dark chocolate that contains 67 percent cocoa is not an acceptable substitute for 72 percent. It just isn't.

Driving

The option to choose exactly what she wants at that very moment will always be your driving child's favorite treat. You may be 100 percent certain that you know exactly what she wants. As long as it's "the option to choose exactly what she wants," you're right on target. With her, ask first and then deliver.

Amiable

Avoiding inconvenience for loved ones is a primary value for your amiable child. So *what* you get her is less important than *how* you give it to her. If she feels that you went to a lot of trouble, the treat is ruined. A simple "I thought of you when I saw this" allows her to fully enjoy her special treatment even if you did drive well out of your way to get it.

Connection
13

Shower Your Kid with Grace

Try This

Give your kid grace even when he or she doesn't deserve it.

Making the Connection

There will be times in your child's life when it's easy to encourage her. She studied hard for a spelling test and got a great grade, or your son put his shoes away in the cubby without being asked. That's when "Great job!" and "Way to go, buddy!" just roll off the tongue.

But the Christ-like parenting we are all aiming for requires a deeper level of encouragement for our kids.

Our kids are going to fail. They are going to disappoint us. They are going to disobey us. And we need to figure out what we're going to say when that happens.

As my mom and I were doing our back-to-school shopping when I was about to enter fourth grade, I asked—well, actually begged—her for a blue satin baseball jacket. I thought I was going to look so cool. But we were beyond tight on money. My dad had been laid off from the electronics firm where he worked, and my mom was performing daily miracles to keep our family financially afloat. But I used my best persuasion techniques to let my mom know in no uncertain terms that I would die—*die!*—if I didn't have The Jacket. I knew my life would change if only I could have it. Everyone would stop in the halls and say, "Wow, look at Kathi!" The cutest boy in the school would ask to sit next to me at lunch, and then ask me to go roller-skating with him on Saturday.

I had built up a rich fantasy life for myself.

So my mom performed another miracle and got me The Jacket. I wore it daily for the first couple weeks of school. Then, on a sweltering day, I took my jacket off to play foursquare. I won the game and floated back to class on a victory high. Everything was going right for ol' Kathi.

Just as the teacher was starting up our science filmstrip, my stomach leapt to my throat. I'd left the blue satin jacket on the bench on the playground!

Again, I went into begging mode. "Please, Mrs. Burkowski, I *have* to get my jacket. You have to let me go." But Mrs. Burkowski wasn't budging. I'd have to wait until recess until I could go get my precious blue jacket.

Recess finally arrived—but my jacket was nowhere to be found. I checked every classroom, the office, and the lost and found. It was gone. At first I was sad that I no longer had my jacket, but the sadness soon turned into panic: I was going to have to tell my mother.

So when I got home that afternoon and my mom saw me without my jacket, I did the only thing that seemed reasonable at the time. I lied. "Oh, I left it in the coat closet."

For two weeks I "forgot" to bring home the jacket. But the lies had to get more complex. I had hung up "Reward" posters all over the school and forgot about them until my mom and I approached my classroom for Back-to-School Night. I roped in some friends to tear down the ones that were posted around the school and to stand in front of the signs taped on the inside of the office windows as my mom and I walked by.

Finally, the jig was up.

The next day my mom drove me to school and told me in no uncertain terms, "Go get the jacket and bring it out to the car." And that's when I broke down in tears and told her I couldn't. The jacket was gone.

My mom, seeing how upset I was, said, "We'll talk about it after school" before she drove off.

I knew I had only until 3:00 that day, and then my mom was going to kill me. It was the longest, and the shortest, day of my nine-year-old life.

Three o'clock came, and I went out to my mom's car. She was there, with a frog-shaped cupcake, and simply said, "I love you."

I don't remember what my punishment was for lying (and trust me, I know there was one). All I remember is that on the day I felt like the worst person in the world, my mom said she loved me. And that said it all.

Make Connecting Fun

Here's my challenge for you this week: Give your child a warm shower of grace the next time he or she deserves anything but.

It's pretty simple. Let's say, for example, that your daughter Kimberly decided to make a mural on her bedroom wall in permanent marker three days before you were to move out of the house. (Not that I would know about that from experience or anything.)

You have three options in your response. You can:

1. *Give your kid justice.* Ground her until she's twenty-seven and make her spend the rest of her childhood scrubbing your walls until they shine.

2. *Give your kid mercy.* Explain to her that while she deserves to be grounded permanently, you're going to let it pass just this one time as long as she helps you paint.

3. *Give your kid grace.* Take her out for ice cream, shower her with love, and explain to her that while she sometimes makes poor (as in *really* poor) choices, your love is unconditional. Then go home and clean up the mess together.

The next time your kid does something less than kosher, I want you to choose option 3. Give your kid grace—just as Christ so freely gave us grace when we didn't deserve it.

Make Connecting Work

I have a giant disclaimer here: It's not always appropriate to lead with grace. For example, if your child does something unsafe, such as riding her bike without a helmet, it's probably not a good time to say, "Oh, well, come inside and have some cookies because I love you anyway." Truth and grace have to live side by side. Choose a time where your child stands to be stunned by your grace—but also to learn from it.

Teen Challenges

You will have ample opportunities to show grace to your teens. And this is probably the hardest age to show that grace to. I'm not saying there shouldn't be consequences for your teen's actions, but we need to balance justice with grace, especially in situations where it's not a matter of disobedience but of immaturity. Just because your sixteen-year-old son is six foot doesn't mean he's an adult.

Step It Up

It's a simple rule in our family—the bio parent punishes, the stepparent doles out grace. It doesn't always work out 100 percent of the time, but it's the rule we try to live by and it works. Never make the stepparent the bad guy.

Suggestions for Singles

When I was single, I remember confusing *grace* for *permissiveness*. I figured since my kids were going through a hard time, I didn't want them angry with me. And let's be honest, I didn't want to be seen as the Mean Parent. But while permissiveness always backfired, grace never did.

I also talked to my kids about the need for grace while I navigated the new, murky waters of being a single parent. This wasn't to give them authority over me; this was to explain that while we were all going through this difficult time, we needed grace on all fronts.

Connecting with Each Personality

Expressive

Your expressive child is likely quite skilled at using subtle manipulation to get what he wants. Don't waste grace when he's merely turning on the charm. The time to turn on the grace is when he makes a complete fool of himself for the girl he likes, gets rejected cold, and needs to be reminded that no matter what, he is loved.

Analytical

Because your analytical child strives for perfection, she lives with constant disappointment. Either she fails to reach that mark of 100 percent (or beyond!) or she reaches it only to fall back. When you enter into her disappointment and offer the gift of grace, you help her see that imperfection is not synonymous with unworthiness.

Driving

If you apply grace in the midst of a driving child-versus-parent control clash, he may mistakenly assume he's the winner and you're a weakling. A far better time to deliver grace aplenty is when your child is blindsided by personal failure. Your offering of grace teaches that his value as a human being is far greater than his achievements as a "human doing."

Amiable

With your amiable child, who has probably refined procrastination to an art form, it's tempting to mistake *rescuing* for *grace*. But grace doesn't jump in and prevent the natural consequences of, say, waiting to start a ten-page paper until the night before it's due. Grace says, "When you receive the low grade you've earned by your choices, I'll still value you as my beloved son."

Just Do Something

Try This

Just do something with your kid.

Making the Connection

Have you ever been caught up in a schedule rut? You know, when you wake up, go to work, do some stuff, come home, do some more stuff, eat dinner, go to bed, lather, rinse, repeat. And before you realize it, you've gone two weeks without doing anything *different*. Or fun. Or relational.

Kimberly loves shoe shopping. OK, so that might be me, but I've taught her well. So when I realized a few months ago that between drama practice and my book deadline, we'd hardly talked for weeks, I decided that drastic times called for drastic measures.

We went shoe shopping. And I'm not talking about one of those "run into Target and grab the first pair of flip-flops in your size" shopping trips. We went to DSW (one of the few places that can shoe my size 11 gunboats) and tried on every pair of boots, pumps, and wedges they had. The good. The bad. And even once, the thigh-high and furry. We tried them on and then strutted around the store doing our own mini fashion show. And laughed more than we had in weeks. (And we may have bought a few pairs—on sale—as souvenirs of our day together.)

Make Connecting Fun

Just doing something—anything—together to break up the routine, can do wonders for your relationships. Think about date night. It can regenerate a relationship, can't it? Same goes for your kids. Just doing something with them (call it a mini kid date if you want) can revive your connection. Make sure you take the time to just do something with your kids from time to time.

20 Things That You Can "Just Do" with Your Kids Today

1. Netflix a movie that your child will love and that you will love just as much simply watching your child laugh or sing along. Have it waiting for him when he gets home. Be sure to pop some popcorn to make the evening complete.

2. Go on a walk together.

3. Make a snack—a cheese plate, some apples with caramel dip, homemade cookies—and share it together.

4. Ask your kid who and what you should be praying for, and then spend some time praying (together).

5. Put two movie tickets in an envelope and ask them for a date.

6. Stretch their imagination. Decorate a box to hold cast-off uniforms, jewelry, hats, and shoes to create a treasure chest of dress-up clothes.

7. Play outside together. See who can get the highest on the swings. Try to fly a kite. Go on a bike ride.

8. Make a video recording of yourselves reading a book out loud, singing a song, or doing a short skit.

9. Go to the bookstore and purchase a magazine or book to read together. Or listen to demos from a favorite musician.

10. Take a picture of the two of you and have it framed—one for them and one for you.

11. Write a letter to your kids in a spiral notebook and ask them to write you back. Pass the journal back and forth, sharing thoughts, ideas, and encouragement.

12. Help your kids do their chores. I love you in four words: "You wash, I'll dry."

13. Create a memory. My son and I, both southpaws, would have Lefties' Night Out. For my daughter and me, it's Girls' Night Out. Carving out time for tradition creates a bond.

14. Work together to make a list of the top ten reasons you love each other. Put it on their bedroom door for the family to see.

15. When you're out running errands or driving to soccer practice, make a detour to your favorite coffee shop. Go inside (instead of using the drive-thru) and enjoy a cup at one of their little tables.

16. Create an iTunes playlist of great music, turn it on, and then sing along at the top of your lungs while you cook dinner or do chores together. Everything is more fun with a VeggieTales soundtrack.

17. Schedule a date. One of my friends has a commitment that no matter what's happening in his life, he will always have a ticket on his fridge. What that means is that he's always looking forward to the next time he'll be able to spend some time with his kids.

18. Take your kid out to dinner at his favorite restaurant—even if it's Burger King.

19. Teach your kid how to do something that you love to do. Show her how to make your (almost) world-famous cheese soufflé. Or teach him how to throw a curveball (even if you just learned yourself by watching a YouTube video).

20. Go shopping. Even running errands together can be fun if you make an effort to focus on each other.

Make Connecting Work

But Kathi, you're probably thinking, *I love spending time with my kids, but many days I just can't find the time. Our schedules are crazy!* I'm with you. I remember weeks (OK, months) when my family hardly had time to grab a taco between activities and homework, much less go on special little outings together. But you can make it work. Here are some tips:

Be purposeful with your time. Even if you have only a five-minute window, you can be purposeful and just do something with your kids. Read a poem. Watch a funny video together on YouTube. Pray. Do jumping jacks.

Make your kid feel like a priority. Go out of your way to make sure your kids know just how much you want to "just do something" with them. Send an invitation. Write it in red on your calendar and count down the days. Tell everyone you see (in front of your kid, of course) how excited you are about your upcoming adventure.

Be spur of the moment. Did your friend cancel your coffee date at the last minute? Invite your kid to go instead. Husband have to work late again? Take your kid out to dinner, just the two of you.

Get your kid in on the planning. You don't have to always be the one planning. Ask your kid what he wants to do, and then make it happen.

Teen Challenges

Most teens will go through a time of pulling away. This doesn't indicate that you're a bad parent or that this is how things are going to be for the rest of your relationship. Don't push the connection; just find a natural way to make it happen. Ask them if they want to grab a drive-thru coffee with you. Or if your daughter has a design eye, ask her for help picking out throw pillows. Be cool, be patient, and just be there for when they are ready to reconnect.

Step It Up

If things are still in the super-awkward phase of stepparenting, make this low-key. Sit across the room from them as they watch their favorite TV show. Casually. No agenda. Then you can ask them questions about it later. Taking an interest in what they are interested in is doing something.

Suggestions for Singles

Make sure you regularly have fun with your kids. Schedule in some time that's not about growth and improvement for you or your kid. Just have some plain old, frivolous, no-goal-necessary fun.

Connecting with Each Personality

Expressive

Of the four, your spontaneous expressive child is most likely to jump at the suggestion to "just do something" together. Ask about responsibilities, such as homework, *before* announcing your idea. Or you may find out later that the "oh nothing" that didn't get done while the two of you were enjoying double scoops at Baskin-Robbins is the cause of low grades.

Analytical

Keep in mind that your analytical child's first response to any unexpected change is rarely positive. So give as much advance warning as possible. Specificity helps. "Let's just do something" together is likely to produce consternation. "Let's go grab a double scoop at Baskin-Robbins" is likely to have him heading toward the car.

Driving

Your driving child has already made plans for the next month, quarter, year, and perhaps even decade. So recognize that she may interpret your suggestion, "Let's just do something," as an imposition or even an unreasonable demand on her valuable time. You can't go wrong asking rather than telling her. "Do you have fifteen minutes to grab a double scoop at Baskin-Robbins with me?" is likely to be met with an energetic, "I do now!"

Amiable

Your amiable child's response to the idea of just doing something together is likely to be related to how much energy that something requires. Keep the energy cost low, and he'll willingly join you. Ask for sudden effort, and he'll weigh the pros and cons of spending time with you versus tiring himself out.

Connection
15

An Out-of-the-Box
Family Challenge

Try This

As a family, take on a challenge that will test your boundaries, push your envelope, and make you connect with your kids.

Making the Connection

If you've read any of my other books (*The Husband Project, Happy Habits for Every Couple, The Me Project, The "What's for Dinner?" Solution, The Get Yourself Organized Project*), you know that I'm a Project Girl. I love a good project—something that's a little bit out of the box, something that takes us out of our everyday life and focuses our time, attention, and maybe even our families on a specific goal.

One of my favorite examples is when my friend Shawna Lee Irish decided to do a month-long project that totally took her out of her comfort zone. She wore the same dress every day for a month. An entire month! And she did it all to teach her kids that they don't need everything they want. How cool is that? Here's how it worked (in Shawna's own words):

> Last year, I was convicted that I needed to embark on the October Dress Project. The October Dress Project is an online challenge that, according to the website, is "anti-consumerism, pro-simplicity, anti-conformity,

pro-imagination." This entailed wearing the same dress every day during the entire month. Because my children are in elementary school, I decided to include them in my project and allow them to learn with me. Katie and Topher became very interested in how we lived with too much. Both of them told their friends about what their mama was doing, and Katie even started wearing the same jeans and shirt every day for a few days. They enjoyed being a part of my daily photos, and when we decided to use the month to pare down our excess belongings via donations and a yard sale, they were happy to purge.

I think that doing the Project with my children made them more aware of *want versus need*. If Mama could wear the same dress every single day for an entire month, saying "I don't have anything to wear" wasn't an option anymore. Like my daughter said, "My feet are warm, my body is covered, we're blessed!" And she began to give her excess away to others. It was a great way to continue the family conversation about others that are in need. That's how I want to raise my children.

But the biggest benefit was that it brought us closer together as a family, and it helped us think about others more than ourselves. We will be working on a way to do the project all together next year as well.

I just love how Shawna took on a challenge that not only took her way, way out of her comfort zone but also used the challenge as a way to get closer to her kids and teach them about something that was important to her.

Make Connecting Fun

Need ideas? Here are several to get you thinking:

- Don't watch TV for thirty days.
- Don't eat out for thirty days.

- Walk every day for thirty minutes.
- Have a family time once a week for a year.
- Have a Facebook-free week.
- For a year, only buy (or wear) clothing produced by people being paid fair wages.
- Sell something around the house on eBay every day for a month to put toward a family vacation.
- Read a book a week for three months.
- Read a certain number of words in a month.
- Support a child through Compassion International (and everyone contributes).
- Cook a new dish every day for thirty days.
- Memorize ten Bible verses in ten days.
- Train for (and participate in) a fun run, walk, or bike ride.
- Walk or bike to school or work for a week.
- Purge one hundred (or two or three hundred) items from your house and donate them to charity.
- Volunteer for one hour a week for a year.
- Purchase only locally produced food for a month.

Make Connecting Work

Something about pushing yourselves to reach a goal as a family will bring you closer together. But the emotions surrounding a challenging situation can also put strain on your family dynamic. Here are a few tips on how to get close and stay close as you endeavor to step outside the box:

Rely on each other. When you are in unusual or uncomfortable territory, you tend to rely on those around you for support, encouragement, and accountability.

Pray for each other. Pray regularly that each and every member of your family will grow and learn more about themselves and God as they complete the challenge.

Talk about your feelings. Spend time each day talking about how the challenge is affecting you—both positively and negatively—and allow your kids to share their feelings as well.

Talk about your struggles. Doing something outside of your comfort zone is bound to be a little uncomfortable, so share your struggles with your kids so they can see that their struggles are normal.

Even if you mess up, don't give up. There are bound to be bumps in the road—so if you slip up, address your mistake, discuss what happened, and keep chugging ahead.

Teen Challenges

Teens, for the most part, are not known for embracing a challenge. Unless it's something they are already passionate about, it may be more of a challenge to get them on board. I know that whenever I suggested change for the sake of change, I was met with resistance. Think of your teens' higher calling; perhaps they would like to raise funds for the theater group at school or for a well in Africa. Find the cause that gets them up in the morning (even if their morning starts at 11:30!).

Step It Up

If your stepson is into sports, ask him to help you get out and walk each day. Is your stepdaughter a gourmet cook wannabe? Then try cooking a new food every night for a week. Capitalize on what already interests them and work on this together.

Suggestions for Singles

This would be a great time to mobilize with another parent to keep you on track. It will be more fun for the kids and more fun for you to have an adult to share the responsibilities with.

Connecting with Each Personality
Expressive

Let your expressive child know that the family will be relying on him for daily encouragement, especially if you've taken on a long-term project. Invite him to find creative ways to boost everyone's spirits along the way: music, balloons, banners, Facebook updates, and so on.

Analytical

Once your family has agreed on the project, your analytical child will keep track of the specifics and let you know when you're getting off track. Invite her to create a blog to chronicle your family's project journey. While she'll shy away from the spotlight, she'll recognize the accountability value of going public.

Driving

"Let's *do* this thing!" is your driving child's clarion call. His drive to produce results will move your family project forward. He'll be eager to regularly put the stars on the chart, stickers on the calendar, fill in the rising thermometer—anything to document progress toward the goal.

Amiable

You can count on your steady amiable child to keep your family focused on the *why* of your project. When the going gets rough, and everyone (even your amiable!) wants to throw in the towel, her quiet reminder of the intrinsic *value* of what you've chosen to do will help everyone get back on track together.

Just the Two of Us

Try This

Do something one-on-one with your kid.

Making the Connection

Yes, it's easier to do things as a family. If you have two kids, you get twice the bonding in the same amount of time. Chalk that up in the win column for a busy parent!

But occasional one-on-one activities with each of your kids can form a connection that goes beyond the everyday and into the extraordinary. My son claims he doesn't remember much of family vacations and activities, but he will never forget the times we spent at coffee shops, just the two of us, talking about writing.

It takes planning, money, and time to do "just the two of us" activities with your kids—and I admit there have been times that I've wondered if it's worth it. Yet, those seem to be the days when my daughter calls to ask my advice about a problem she's having at work or texts to see if I can meet her for coffee just to talk. And with a chuckle, I realize all of my effort has created a deep, lasting bond that will keep our family connected for years to come.

And that makes it all worth it.

Make Connecting Fun

Go Big

Take your kid on a one-on-one vacation. My friend Kim and her husband had long promised their children that when each child turned sixteen, he or she would go on an extended vacation with one of the parents; their daughter would go with Mom and their son with Dad. The only requirements were that it had to be in the continental U.S. and the kids had to help plan the trip.

"Money was tight, and we had to give up a lot in order to afford the vacations," Kim says, "but we knew how important it was to spend that time with each of the kids." Time alone with a parent during the teen years can be just the ticket for a teenager who needs to be reminded that she'll always have a safe haven as she moves out into the world.

If an extended vacation is impossible, try a long weekend with each of your children, as my friend Lynn did. She and her husband, Mark, have taken turns going on a weekend getaway with their boys, Jake and Ben. Lynn got the first opportunity when each of their sons turned ten, and Mark two years later when the boys turned twelve. Lynn says the best part about the trips was getting to see the uniqueness of each of her boys. While Ben wanted to get dressed up and go to the area culinary academy to try new and exotic dishes, Jake was thrilled to pedal across northern California on a guided bike tour with Lynn bringing up the rear.

Finally, if a weekend away won't work, an overnighter in a local hotel or campground can go a long way toward strengthening the bond between you and your child.

Go Medium

Take your kid on a regular "just the two of us" date night. Justen and I began this tradition when he was seven years old, and we still do it now that he's out of high school. About once a month, we choose a night to go out on the town, just the two of us. It may be hamburgers and chocolate shakes at the fifties-style diner in town, picking up mystery novels and hot chocolate at our favorite bookstore, or going to a coffee shop to hang out. Whatever the activity, it gives us a chance to talk without the distraction of the phone, his siblings, or the TV.

To create your own "just the two of us" date night, ask your child what type of activity he'd enjoy. Maybe you both love Japanese food and want to try out the new sushi restaurant in town. Maybe you're astronomy fans; take a star walk sponsored by a local planetarium. The object of your evening is to get out of the house and do something you will both enjoy and can talk about in the years to come.

Go Small (but Significant)

Connect with your kid over small but memorable activities. When Kimberly was eight, we started sharing a mother-daughter journal. One night she would lay it on my nightstand for me to write in; the next, I would tuck it under her pillow for her to record her thoughts and dreams. Through the pages of that little book, we've shared secrets, settled arguments, and discussed life. It's been a great way to talk about all the fun and not-so-fun issues going on in my little girl's life. It has also given me the opportunity to share Bible verses, advice, and love notes in a nonthreatening way.

It's easy to get the ball rolling on a parent-child journal. Find a notebook, attach a pen, and then write a question to start the conversation. Ask about school, friends, books, or anything else that interests your child. Ask open-ended questions such as, "Tell me about the best book you've read in fourth grade." This will help you get more in-depth responses, as well as having even more to write about the next time you share journal entries.

Make Connecting Work

As I said earlier, planning a great one-on-one connection with your kid takes time, money, and creativity. Creativity? That you have. Time and money? Not so much. Here are a few ways to make planning easier, faster, and less expensive:

Make a one-on-one vacation jar. Decorate a jar or box and use it to save for your next big one-on-one adventure. Tape on the jar a picture of where you and your child want to go, and then put it somewhere where the two of you can see it. Drop spare change into it whenever you can.

Keep a list of ideas taped to the fridge. Work together to make a list of all the things you'd like to do together and then you'll never be at a loss for ideas when the opportunity presents itself. Add to the list whenever either of you has a new idea.

Go for free or cheap. Not all one-on-one adventures are expensive. Go to a local gallery opening to check out a new artist. Listen to live music in a local café. Take a picnic to the park. Cook dinner together. Play a game. Go on a bike ride. Shoot hoops at the YMCA. There are lots of fun things you can do together that cost hardly anything.

Keep your eyes open for deals. Check Groupon or Living Social for deals on getaways, tickets, and activities you can do with your kid.

Be spontaneous. Not every one-on-one adventure has to be planned in advance. Be spontaneous! On your way home from school, stop for frozen yogurt. On a sunny afternoon, head out for a walk in the park. On one of those days when you have nothing in your cupboards for dinner, take your kid to your favorite diner.

Teen Challenges

I found that with my teens, watching movies was the best way to connect one-to-one. It was great to have something to talk about that didn't focus on grades or a messy room. Something about loving (or hating) a movie together can really bond you!

Step It Up

One-on-one with your stepkid might be a stretch depending where you are in your relationship. I think the better way to look at this connection is to bond with one kid at a time, even if it involves both you and your spouse.

Suggestions for Singles

I bet you feel that you have more than enough time with your kids. But remember, the point is to connect with one of your kids. If you have two or more kids, make sure you do something one-on-one with each child—not all in one week, but as you can. Maybe have dinner with your daughter while your son is at scouts or a snack with your son while your daughter's at dance.

Connecting with Each Personality

Expressive

One-on-one time is a great chance to meet your expressive child's need for physical connection. With respect for age boundaries, you might try holding hands, walking arm-in-arm (or pinky-to-pinky), ruffling her hair, or giving her a pressure-point hand or neck massage.

Analytical

Approach just-the-two-of-us time with your analytical child like a journalist. Take along a pad of paper, a pen, and a list of questions (see Connection 10 for ideas). Your goal is to learn key details about him without coming across as an interrogator. Spend your time together *noticing* his likes, dislikes, mannerisms, and quirks. And jot it all down so you'll remember.

Driving

Consider taking your driving child to an event normally reserved for adults, such as a Shakespeare play, a memoir writing seminar, or a photography show. You'll want to match the event to her interests and skills, of course, and set her up for success by laying a solid foundation ahead of time. She'll leave more energized than ever about pursuing her goals because you so clearly believe in her ability to handle complexity.

Amiable

What you do for just-the-two-of-us time with your amiable child is far less important than *how* you do it. If you start shouting at the lousy drivers on the way to your special time together, he'll wish you'd both stayed home where there was no traffic…and no shouting. Choose to make his need for peace your highest priority for the outing. And you may be surprised by how peaceful *you* feel when you get home!

Connection
17

Have a Game Night

Try This

Have a family game night.

Making the Connection

It was 9:45 on a Thursday night and we had to keep reminding the kids to keep their voices down. (We live in a townhouse and our neighbors aren't always as interested in our conversation as we are.) But it was hard to keep down the general ruckus.

Justen had just turned twenty-one, and everyone was over to celebrate. He had already had his "friend party" at one of his favorite restaurants, but tonight was his family party with his grandparents, a favorite aunt, his cousin Elsa, and his three siblings (along with assorted significant others). After the steaks had been eaten, the presents opened, and the bistro chocolate cake served, all the kids settled in for the highlight of the evening: cards.

Our family likes to play together. Whether it's board games, the card game *Uno*, or Rock Band on the Wii, whenever we get together, there is some kind of game involved.

Having a family "go-to" game is a great way to put aside chores, homework, and sisterly squabbles for an hour or so and connect as a family. It gives everyone the chance to disconnect from their technology—yes, even Mom and Dad—and connect to each other.

At least a couple of Sunday nights a month, we have all the kids over for dinner, and when schedules allow, we follow it up with a game night. Playing together has bonded our blended family, and the kids love to tell the tales of their board game conquests, the times we were stranded in the snow together with nothing more than a couple decks of cards, and the time that Mom totally lost her cool when Amanda stole one of her gun cards while playing *Bang!*

I don't think I can overstate the effect having fun together has had on blending our families and connecting us all together. Last night, my daughter and I were out running some errands, and I asked her about what she thought it took to really connect her with her stepbrother and sister. (I love doing book research on the way to Target.) She said that although she and her stepbrother, Jeremy, had known each other for years and had lived together once Roger and I were married, it wasn't until we started playing board and card games together that she really started to enjoy him as a person.

I'm willing to break out a heated game of *Yahtzee* for a closer family. How about you? So for this challenge, I want you to plan a big, loud, disturb-the-neighbors-at-9:45 game night.

Make Connecting Fun

Picture this: the pizza fondue is simmering in its pot. There are fancy root beers on ice and stacks of game boxes and decks of cards decorate the hutch in our kitchen. Roger's made his salsa (and no one cares that it really doesn't go with pizza fondue), and the dog is hiding under the kitchen table. The kids are back at home and the volume has risen to inappropriate levels.

That's what family game night looks like at the Hunter-Lipp house. Here are a few of the games we love to play:

Code Names	*Uno*
EuroRails	*Life*
Monopoly	*Sorry*
Apples to Apples	*Yahtzee*
Pictionary	*Hand and Foot Canasta*
Jenga	*Nertz*

Make Connecting Work

Here are some things to consider when planning out a game night:

Make it an event. Establish one night a month as game night. Let your kids know it's going to be an event. Make something light for dinner and have a few family favorite snacks throughout the night.

Mix it up. Have a couple of games that allow the number of people to change. If you play games that have only a certain number of people, it will be harder for your kids to invite their friends over to join in.

Keep in mind your kids' ages and stages. Unless you're a parent of multiples, your kids are probably at different ages and different skill levels, so it helps to pull out the games that mostly rely on the draw of a card or the roll of the dice to determine the winner. It can be frustrating for little kids to always be mismatched in a game knowing they are going to lose each and every time.

Have a variety of games. Dedicate an area of your home to games that don't plug in. A few board games, a few card games, maybe *Jenga* for a little something different thrown in.

Don't be afraid to go high tech. Use the Wii or Kinect to have a family dance competition, or get out your iPad and download the apps for *Battleship* or *Uno*.

Teen Challenges

If you've never had a family game night, don't mandate that from now on, every Friday will be Family Game Night and it's carved in stone and the only way for your teenager to get out of it is with a doctor's note. That's not the path to family bonding. Make it fun, make it irresistible. We've even given away an iTunes gift card (of five whole dollars) to the winner of our game tournament.

Suggestions for Singles

When I was a single mom, I did my best to engage with my son by playing video games with him. (He still teases me about getting motion sickness trying to fly a helicopter on an Xbox.) If you need some good side-by-side time where your child can relax and not have the expectation of connecting, come alongside her in a game she already enjoys.

Step It Up

Let your stepkids teach you their favorite game instead of introducing them to one of yours. Their game is something they are already comfortable with.

While we were in the midst of blending, we created a night with all the kids' favorite goodies and some games that each family liked. (As a blended family, we had to approach with caution.) So along with pizza and appropriate snacks, we asked Roger's kids to teach us their favorite card game, *German Bridge*, and we introduced them to some of our family favorites.

Our first game night went well. We found that some games were entirely too long (*Empire Builder*) for a fast-and-fun game night, but a quick game of *Bang!* was perfect for some back-and-forth fun (and it was easy to eat chips while playing).

Connecting with Each Personality

Expressive

Your expressive child will enjoy interpretive games, such as *Pictionary* and *Taboo*, in which rules are minimal and communication is the goal. His natural verbal skills will help him excel at such games, and you may need to coach him to recognize that other family members may find word-based games quite challenging.

Analytical

Avoid games with thick rule books; your analytical child will want to read, memorize, and follow every single instruction. But do be consistent with the rules for whatever game you choose. Either "table talk" is always allowed or it never is. Either everyone can pick up a card when they change their mind or no one can. Your analytical child needs to know what to expect.

Driving

Although most games involve a winner and a loser, your driving child is likely to be drawn to games that involve total demolition of the enemy. Encourage her to engage in world domination at a time other than family game night. Help her learn the vital skills of being a gracious winner…and a gracious loser.

Amiable

Your amiable child's main concern during family game night will be the feelings of every other family member. His favorite game would be one in which everybody wins and nobody can lose. Since this is not a practical option, he may make "mistakes" or even lose on purpose, especially if an analytical or driving sibling is becoming upset. Help him realize that he is not responsible for other family members' reactions, nor is his self-sacrifice actually helpful, or healthy, in the long run.

Connection
18

Cook Together

Try This

Cook a meal (or snack or dessert) with your kids.

Making the Connection

I thought my days of "extreme cooking" were behind me.

You see, I've been preparing and freezing meals most of my adult life. With first two and then four kids to feed after Roger and I got married, when dinner was an afterthought, I was the one who paid the price.

But now Roger and I almost have a kid-free house. Yes, I still plan out our meals. And I even still freeze meals for those busy nights when I know we both have busy days and want to avoid the lure of convenient fast food. But for the most part, I was happy to retire from the big cooking days that were a matter of survival when my kids were young.

And then I got to thinking (always a dangerous thing). Both our girls were living on their own—Amanda working full-time at a child care facility and Kimber going to school full-time plus working part-time at a clothing consignment store as well as several hours a week for me. They were just as tired as I was when they got home at night, and I knew that both of them wanted to eat healthy. So I thought I would make them an offer: Come over and cook with me one night a month. We'll decide on a menu ahead of time, make as many meals as we can, and divide them up.

I wasn't sure how receptive they would be to the idea. Cooking together? Would it just feel like another chore?

I was pretty certain Kimber would be receptive because we have cooked together all our lives. But Amanda (who moved out of the house about the time I married Roger) and I had cooked together only for the occasional celebratory dinner or holiday. I just didn't know if she would want to do it. So I prayed before I asked. There is just something that bonds people over preparing food together. Everyone has a job (chopping veggies, browning hamburger, packaging up the dinners), but all of those little jobs come together to make a great meal. I knew we would have a great time, if I could just get her interested.

Turns out, I underestimated the power of being broke. Both girls jumped on the chance for some cook-ahead, home cooked meals that they could just pop in the oven (or microwave) at the end of a long day.

So we created cooking lists and shopping lists and doled out jobs. After just a couple of hours we had twenty-three meals to divvy up for our respective homes.

While your kids may not be old enough to enjoy the benefits of extreme cooking for their own homes, most kids enjoy eating. I've found that cooking together with kids, and then eating the results, is one of the best ways to connect regularly with your kids.

Make Connecting Fun

Extreme cooking aside—which you can read about more in *The "What's for Dinner?" Solution*—there are lots of ways to bond with your kids over cooking. After all, nothing (OK, almost nothing) binds two people together tighter than chopping, peeling, cutting, and boiling their way to something delicious and then indulging in it together. Here are easy ways that you can connect over cooking with kids of all ages.

If your kids are preschoolers:

- Pull up a stool while you're cooking dinner and explain what you're doing while they watch.

- Purchase one of those plastic cake-cutting knives (at any home superstore) and let your kid practice cutting soft foods like lettuce, pears, and mozzarella cheese.

- Let your kids sniff the spices as you add them to a dish, telling you what they think of the smell.

- Have your kids close their eyes and sample the ingredients as you add them to your dish. You might even get them to inadvertently try a tomato or—gasp!—something green.

- Look through cookbooks (preferably ones with big, mouthwatering pictures) with your kids and let them pick out recipes they want to try.

If your kids are grade-schoolers:

- Get your kids their own measuring cups and let them practice measuring various amounts. (Bonus: you can tell your kid's teacher that you've been helping your kid practice using fractions at home.)

- Pick up smaller-sized whisks, rubber spatulas, and wooden spoons, and let your kids join in on all of the whisking, scraping, and stirring.

- Give your kid the title of sous-chef and have him read you the ingredient list while you pull the items out of the pantry. Or have him read the instructions as you carry them out.

- Work together to plan a special meal for the family. Choose the recipes, write a list, do the shopping, and do the cooking together.

If your kids are middle- and high-schoolers:

- Flip the roles and make yourself the sous-chef and your kid the head chef. Let him boss you around the kitchen.

- Challenge your kid to create her own recipes. Ask her if she thinks almond extract would be a good replacement for vanilla in the cookies. Or see if she wants to try cumin or paprika in her scrambled eggs.

- Plan a dinner party for some of your kid's friends.
- Make homemade bread. It sounds complicated, I know, but it's actually pretty hard to mess up—even for kids. And you'll end up with a great-smelling house and a warm loaf for dinner.

Make Connecting Work

I love to cook—don't get me wrong—but I especially love to cook when I have gadgets around that make cooking easier and more fun.

Eight Awesome Gadgets that Make Cooking with Kids Fun

1. *A mini slow cooker.* Cook a small batch of applesauce at night, and then serve it warm to your kids for breakfast. Or let your kid keep their pizza fondue (recipe in Connection 2) warm in their own pot.

2. *Pampered Chef Apple Peeler/Corer/Slicer.* I'm pretty sure no one gets more giddy than I do to see an apple peeled, cored, and sliced in one twist of the wrist—except for maybe Kimber. And the fact that it is so fun and makes it so easy to make Apple Brown Betty…well, you can see why I get giddy.

3. *An egg slicer.* Even kids who can't handle a knife can easily slice strawberries, mushrooms, avocados, and yes, even eggs.

4. *A (really cute) apron stocked with cooking gear.* Pick up a cute apron (some of my favorites are at www.kidscookingshop .com) and fill the pockets with small-sized spatulas, whisks, plastic knives, and more so your kid has easy access to all their cooking tools.

5. *Pampered Chef Cut-N-Seal.* After explaining to Justen 452 times that the crust of bread is OK to eat, I finally gave up and got myself a Cut-N-Seal. It cuts off the crusts *and*

seals the edges, turning any sandwich into a delicious little pocket of, well, whatever you put inside the sandwich. I use it for myself now. And no one is going to convince me that crust is OK to eat.

6. *A one-egg fry pan.* Kids can help you fry up eggs and Canadian bacon to make their own Egg Not-McMuffins at home…and you won't have to spend five minutes using a commercial-grade scrubber to get a giant pan clean.

7. *A homemade ice-cream maker.* I know it's nostalgic and fun to carefully layer rock salt and ice and then crank out ice cream by hand, but with a handy countertop ice-cream maker, you can whip up homemade frozen yogurt for breakfast. Or toss together a quick sorbet as an after-dinner treat. Or make double-fudge rocky road even when it's raining outside. Definitely worth the investment.

8. *A doughnut maker.* My friend Rachel picked up a doughnut maker for her son's eighth birthday a few months ago, and he gets up early in the morning before school to make himself doughnuts and bagels for breakfast. And it's a lot healthier than a trip through the doughnut drive-thru. They whip up whole-wheat and sugar-free batter all the time, and since it's baked, not fried, it actually makes for a (kind of) healthy breakfast.

Teen Challenges

Perfect a recipe together. I love a good fudgy brownie. So a few years ago, Kimber and I set out to make the ultimate fudge brownies. We made our favorite recipe, then added a little of this, subtracted a little of that, until it was just perfect. It took some trial and error, but I chalked it up to my quest to connect. (And having an endless supply of almost-perfect brownies on hand wasn't too shabby either.)

Step It Up

Let your stepkids introduce you to some of their favorite foods. If they know how to make them, great! Then they can teach you. If not, find a recipe online and create their favorites.

Suggestions for Singles

If money is tight, instead of having fancy food for meals, why not mix up the times? Have waffles for dinner or ham-and-cheese paninis for breakfast. Everyone cooks, everyone eats.

Connecting with Each Personality

Expressive

For your expressive child, cooking is all about how artistic everything *looks* when it's done. (If it tastes good, that's a bonus!) From making pear-half bunny rabbit salads (with almond-slice ears, cinnamon-candy nose, and cottage-cheese tail) to high-class cupcake creations, plan to have fun being creative in the kitchen with this child.

Analytical

Your time in the kitchen with your analytical child can't start until you've poured through a Pampered Chef catalog and toured Williams Sonoma together, looking at cooking paraphernalia. (You know the rule: to do the job right, you need the right tool.) Once in the kitchen, realize that recipes will be followed to the nth degree. Don't even think of uttering the phrases "a little of this" or "a little of that."

Driving

Recipes for one-dish meals requiring five ingredients or less will appeal to your driving child. So will a food processor: it's powerful and fast, just like her. Efficiency is the goal, so time spent on once-a-month cooking is worthwhile; time spent making fancy garnishes is unfathomable.

Amiable

Your amiable child will appreciate—to the point of devotion— kitchen gadgets with labor-saving qualities. Turn the handle of the

Apple Peeler/Corer/Slicer rather than using a paring knife and potato peeler? Sure thing! Push the button on the Salad Shooter rather than muscling cheese up and down against a grater? You bet! If he can expend minimal energy, still get credit for cooking, and end up with something worth eating, life is sweet.

Connection
19

Pray for Your Kids

Try This

Start a prayer journal to help you intentionally pray for your kids.

Making the Connection

A few years ago, Amanda was engaged to someone who wasn't right for her. It was obvious to Roger and me, and everything in me wanted to open my mouth and talk some sense into her. I wanted to explain what I thought. I wanted to beg and plead. I wanted to write out a list of all the godly characteristics that I envisioned for her future spouse. But I didn't. Instead, we shut up and prayed.

And we prayed.

And we prayed.

And we prayed some more.

It took almost a year (yes, an entire year!), but they broke off the engagement. We now joke that if your kid is dating someone who isn't right for them, call us. We have a ministry of praying the wrong guys out.

All joking aside, praying for your kids is powerful. I can say without hesitation that it is the number one most valuable thing I have done for my children. And that's why I want to encourage you to start a prayer journal that will help you intentionally pray for your kids every day.

Make Connecting Fun

Starting a prayer journal is actually really easy.

Step 1: Pick up a journal. I like mine to be small enough to fit into my purse so I can bring it with me when I'm traveling and pretty enough to display on a bookshelf. But really, anything—from a 99-cent spiral notebook from the dollar store to an iPad with a stylus—will work.

Step 2: Pick a time to journal. If you're anything like me, you probably start every day with the best intentions. But by the time you've managed to feed the kids, walk the dog, make the coffee, do carpool, clean the dishes, sweep the floor, *and* switch the laundry (all before 9:00 a.m.) even your best laid plans get derailed. So set aside time every day—set a daily reminder on your iPhone if you have to—so that praying for your kids becomes a daily priority.

Step 3: Talk to God on paper. Your prayers don't have to be eloquent or full of poetic language. Just talk to God about your kids. One thing I've found to be really helpful is to use a verse from the Bible to pray for my kids. Here are a few of the verses I've prayed over my kids over the years:

> Do not conform to the pattern of this world, but be transformed by the renewing of your mind. Then you will be able to test and approve what God's will is—his good, pleasing and perfect will (Romans 12:2).

> But grow in the grace and knowledge of our Lord and Savior Jesus Christ. To him be glory both now and forever! Amen (2 Peter 3:18).

> May integrity and uprightness protect me,
>   because my hope, LORD, is in you
>   (Psalm 25:21).

> Let love and faithfulness never leave you;
>   bind them around your neck,
>   write them on the tablet of your heart
>   (Proverbs 3:3).

> I cling to you;
>   your right hand upholds me
>   (Psalm 63:8).

The tongue has the power of life and death,
   and those who love it will eat its fruit
   (Proverbs 18:21).

Make Connecting Work

I've seen God use the words I've prayed over my kids to protect them, to encourage them, and sometimes even to help them to change course. And when you're keeping a prayer journal, you'll be able to see God's story for your kids' lives unfold in a powerful and prayer-driven way.

My friend Erin's mom has kept a daily prayer journal for each of her kids since they were tiny babies. She has the journals lined up on her bookshelf—more than thirty volumes at this point—and occasionally pulls them out to give her kids a tangible reminder of the power of prayer.

Erin remembers a time when she was really struggling. With three young kids at home, she wondered how she could keep a grasp on herself when her life seemed to be overwhelmed with diapers and runny noses. She confided her feelings to her mom, and her mom went to her bookshelf and pulled out a prayer journal she had written in 1996. Erin read her mom's prayers—prayers that were written long before her kids were born—that motherhood would bring Erin spiritual growth along with an increased reliance on God. How powerful is that?

I want to encourage you to do the same thing—to intentionally and purposefully pray for your kids daily.

Teen Challenges

Your teens are often mature enough to know what they need prayer for. Why not ask them what they need you to pray for? You may be pleasantly stunned by their answers.

Step It Up

With my stepkids, I found that I often ended up praying the same verses for myself as I was praying for them. It gave me empathy for them that I might not otherwise have had.

Suggestions for Singles

Praying for my kids' dad following our divorce was one of the hardest things I ever had to do. But I realized it was imperative; my kids needed a healthy dad as much as they needed a healthy mom.

Connecting with Each Personality

Here are some ideas for prayers you can pray for your kids based on the unique needs of their personality.

Expressive

"Help _____ to realize that you have specifically chosen and appointed him" (John 15:16).

"May ___ sense that she is your handiwork, created anew to do the wonderful things you have planned" (Ephesians 2:10).

Analytical

"Lead _____ to truly know that because of you, he is pure and holy and freed from sin, that he is right with you" (1 Corinthians 1:30).

"Free _____ from anxiety; may she continue to pray, give thanks, and take her needs to you" (Philippians 4:6).

Driving

"May _____ allow Christ to lead him boldly and confidently" (Ephesians 3:12).

"Help _____ to see that she is complete in Christ and to give him full authority in her life" (Colossians 2:10).

Amiable

"Remind ___ that you will keep in perfect peace the one whose mind is steadfast because he trusts in you" (Isaiah 26:3).

"May the peace of God, which transcends all understanding, guard _____'s heart and mind today" (Philippians 4:7).

Connection
20

Love Notes

Try This

Write your kid a love note.

Making the Connection

Back when my kids were younger, we kept a small, lidded basket better known as the "family mailbox" in the middle of our cluttered kitchen counter. And inside it, I'd often find sticky notes with the words "I love you, Mom," written with green glitter pen in my daughter's best nine-year-old cursive.

Our family mailbox was a great way to encourage each other and brighten our kids' days. Even when my kids grew past the age of wanting notes in their brown-paper lunch bags where their friends could see them, they never minded finding a note or a small treat in the family mailbox.

Since then, I've learned that a handwritten and heartfelt note can go a long way to make someone feel loved, cared for, and appreciated. So for this connection, I want you to write your kid a love note and leave it where she'll find it.

Make Connecting Fun

Here are a few ideas to get the ink flowing.

Start a family mailbox. All you need is a basket, a pad of paper, and a pen. You can start the ball rolling by writing notes to each member of your family. You could start with a note of encouragement or maybe a Bible verse. End the note with a question, such as, "If you could be invisible for a day, what would you do?" I promise you will get some fascinating mail in your little basket.

Welcome your kid home with a note. I saw this on Pinterest. Use dry-erase markers to write "Welcome home! I love you!" on a china plate. Then prop up the plate on a plate stand and put it on the counter for your kids to see when they get home from school.

Send notes in your kid's lunch. In her book *Love Notes in Lunchboxes: And Other Ideas to Color Your Child's Day*, Linda Gilden tells about the day her daughter said: "You know, Mom, I don't really remember what you said in all those notes you wrote in my lunches. But I remember you wrote them and they always showed you cared. Some days I think all you said was, 'Have a good day' or 'You are special,' but it meant a lot. Just to know that you took the time to write a note and that you thought it was an important part of my lunch made my day. Most kids only had food in their lunch bags!"

Yes, food is an essential part of the lunchbox. But even more important than the food for our children's bodies is the food for their spirits. And it doesn't have to be dispensed in a lunchbox. There are plenty of ways to encourage and affirm our children.

Write out an acrostic using the letters of your child's name. Hang it on their door or on the fridge so they can see how great you think they are. Here's an example of what I have in mind:

> **J**ust so funny
>
> **E**nergetic
>
> **R**eady for anything
>
> **E**veryone loves him
>
> **M**y favorite person to watch cartoons with
>
> **Y**ou are a great kid!

Send Scripture notes. Can't think of what to write? God gave us a whole book of love notes. Just borrow one of his! Then add a few words of your own.

God's Note: "Look to the LORD and his strength; seek his face always" (1 Chronicles 16:11).

Mom's or Dad's note: Always trust God. He knows what's best for you, and he is bigger than any problem you may have.

Write a list. Jot down a quick list and leave it on a sticky note on the bathroom mirror where your child can see it when they brush their teeth or get ready for school. Try "Top Three Reasons I Love You" or "Top Five Reasons Our Family Is the Greatest" or "Top Five Reasons You Are My Favorite Lunchbox Kid."

Make Connecting Work

Writing love notes can be intimidating. Even I get flustered writing them from time to time, and I've written seven books! But your kids aren't going to care whether you put "*i* before *e* except after *c*." They aren't going to fret about how long your note was or what paper you used or where they found it. They'll just love getting a note from you.

Notes do not have to be long or eloquent or poetic. A few well-chosen words can go a long way. It's not even *what* you say; it's important to say *something!* No matter the age of your children—three, seven, twelve, twenty, or forty-five—a note is a great way to say, "I love you!"

Teen Challenges

Don't, I repeat *don't*, put gushy hearts or stickers on your teen's lunch bag. Been there. Done that. Learned my lesson.

Let your notes be short, sweet, and preferably texts.

Step It Up

Again, your stepchild is not looking for gushy sentiment most of the time. But displaying a good grade on the fridge, with a sticky note that says "Impressive!" is just enough to let them know "I notice what's going on."

Suggestions for Singles

We had a write on/wipe off board where I could leave notes for my kids, and every once in a while, they would leave a note for me. I started to call it the "Love Board," and it was great for my kids, and for me.

Connecting with Each Personality

Expressive

Sentence starters for writing words your expressive child will read and reread:

> "You **inspire** me to…"
>
> "I'm **delighted** to see you…"
>
> "Your **refreshing** perspective on…"
>
> "I admire the **spirit** with which you…"
>
> "You are such a natural **promoter** for…"
>
> "I enjoy hearing you **talk** about…"

Analytical

Sentence starters for writing words your analytical child will read and reread:

> "You are so **faithful** with…"
>
> "I'm inspired by your **idealism** about…"
>
> "Your **considerate** nature…"
>
> "I appreciate your **sensitivity** to…"
>
> "You are so **thoughtful** when…"
>
> "I enjoy the **deep** conversations we have about…"

Driving

Sentence starters for writing words your driving child will read and reread:

> "Your skills of **persuasion**…"
>
> "I admire your **resourcefulness** with…"
>
> "You are an **independent**…"

"I'm envisioning you as a **leader** of…"

"You are so **outspoken** about…"

"I enjoy our friendly **debates** over…"

Amiable

Sentence starters for writing words your amiable child will read and reread:

"You are so **patient** when…"

"I appreciate your **diplomacy** with…"

"Your **consistency** in…"

"I'm proud of your **tolerance** of…"

"You are such a good **friend** to…"

"I enjoy our **bad puns** and **sarcastic comments** about…"

Connection
21

When Are We
Going to Get There?

Try This

Use your minivan time to have purposeful conversations with your kids.

Making the Connection

Do you spend large portions of your life in your car?

I do. Between traveling for work and driving my kids to their various activities, there have been many days in the last eighteen years that I spent more hours behind the wheel than any other activity besides sleeping. And at no time was I in my car more than when I was homeschooling my kids—or "vanschooling" is more like it. We were always on our way to a Bible study, a science lesson at the local church, the American history co-op, or a service project.

I'm sure you've felt this way as well. If you're a stay-at-home parent, I bet you don't spend a ton of time actually at home. If you're a working parent, you may have been tempted upon occasion to keep a pillow and a small blanket in the car.

And here's a secret: That time when you're stuck in the car can be great for your relationship with your kids. Or it can be just another block of time that it takes to get to band practice.

I think we need to be intentional about our time in the car. Yes, there is value to limiting the time we spend running around, but for all those times when a car trip is necessary, why not take advantage of your time together? Here are some of my favorite ways of getting where you need to go and connecting with your kids at the same time. So for this "connection," I want you to think of ways that you can connect with your kids car-style.

Make Connecting Fun

I know what you're thinking right now: *I get it, Kathi. I know I should be working on connecting with my kids in the car and all that, but the truth is, I'm not sure I can stand another minute of license plate bingo or—worse— singsongy kids' CDs. What can I do to make connecting in the car fun—for me* and *for them?* Here are a few (totally non-singsongy) ideas.

Just Talk

Time in the car can seem never-ending. That's why having a goal to get the conversation rolling will make the trip easier for you and your kids.

And trust me, when you have surly teenagers (or not-so-surly grade-schoolers), there are times that keeping the conversation flowing is a lot of work. I can remember several times that I needed to remind my kids as they plunked into their seats and popped headphones over their ears that I wasn't there just to serve their transportation needs. We were a family and we needed to roll like one. I wanted to know about their day, their friends, what they were learning in school. If the I'm-your-mom-and-I-deserve-some-warm-fuzzies guilt trip doesn't get them talking, here are a few good car-time conversation starters:

- If this car could be headed anywhere right now, where would you want to go?

- Describe your ultimate favorite meal.

- If you had to study the same thing all day, every day, what subject would you choose?

- What do you think your friend Johnny is talking about to his parents right now?
- What's one thing you could do to make the world a better place?
- If you could snap your fingers and any person you chose would magically appear in the seat next to you, who would you choose?
- If you could jump into a movie or a book, which one would you choose? How would you change the ending?

It's Story Time

Stories in the car aren't just for keeping toddlers quiet in the backseat. One of the best ways of connecting I've experienced with my kids was to listen to long books as we were driving around.

Most of the time when I was pulling chauffeur duty, my kids and I would talk or I would listen to an audiobook (written for adults, but with nothing that I wouldn't want my kids to hear) while they read books in the back. Then one day, as I was listening to *The Complete Sherlock Holmes*, Justen yelled, "Don't turn off the car!" as I was pulling into the Target parking lot, ready to run errands. I had no idea he'd been listening along with me. So we sat for another five minutes to let him listen to the end of the story.

At first you might be thinking, *How does listening together connect you?* Listening to the same story has given us some great conversation starters. We can talk about why the characters behaved the way they did and what choices we would have made in the same situations.

Adults form book clubs for a reason—they want to talk with others about the details of a book they've read. They are dying to know if the other members of the club felt the same way they did when Mr. Darcy berates poor Elizabeth at the ball. As readers, we don't want to just read a book; we want to discuss it.

Not only have my kids and I discussed books—we've gone so far as to take trips to meet the authors. As I mentioned earlier in Connection 1, Justen, Kimberly, and I became enchanted with a nonfiction story,

The Prize Winner of Defiance, Ohio: How My Mom Raised Ten Kids on Twenty-Five Words or Less. It's the story of an enterprising mother of ten who kept her family afloat by entering jingle contests in the fifties and sixties. Because of her industriousness and way with words, her family won cars, appliances, trips, and hundreds of other prizes, many of which were sold to keep their home and feed their family.

We listened to this set of CDs over and over again. It's a brilliant story and inspiring as well. We loved the rich characters and how the family pulled together to survive.

So imagine how tickled we were to find out that the author, Terry Ryan, was going to be giving a book reading in the nearby town of Santa Cruz. We made a day out of it, eating in a nearby restaurant and then heading over to the bookshop in Santa Cruz to meet the author. My kids were thrilled—especially since they were the only ones in attendance who weren't old enough to drive. They asked questions and got their book signed (yes, we had the CDs and the book) and got to meet a real live author.

One of the keys to listening to books together is to make sure that you move on to chapter books as soon as your kids are old enough to understand them. Books with longer stories are critical for a few reasons:

Not torturing the parents. This is a must. Even the best little kid books wear thin after a while. But books such as the Laura Ingalls Wilder "Little House" series are simple enough for young kids to understand but are so rich in story and detail that they will hold the attention of adults and older siblings as well. And while younger kids may not get every detail, you can always turn the CD off and have a discussion about parts of the story they may not get right away.

Continuing story. I can't tell you how many times my kids wanted to sit in a parked car to finish the chapter of a book. I loved that they were so into a book that going into a friend's house could wait a few minutes. I knew that the story had really captured them. Having a continuing story makes kids want to come back and listen for more.

Book discussion. A shorter story may have only one point, but a chapter book will have many aspects for your family to discuss. As you listen to a book together, you will find out that your kids react to totally different parts of the story.

What to Listen to

We listen to a wide variety of stories, both Christian and secular, fiction and nonfiction. I found that this was the best way to have a conversation with my kids—when an issue was raised in the story, it was a great time to talk about it in a nonthreatening way. Some of the titles I suggest below may seem a little grown-up for younger kids, so use your discretion as you to decide what's appropriate for your family.

It's easier than ever to take stories in the car with you. All you need is an iPod and an Amazon account. We even have downloads of some of our favorite books available for free at our public library.

A great resource for extremely well-produced audio stories is Focus on the Family's Radio Theatre (www.focusonthefamily.com/promos/radio-theatre.aspx). They have done an outstanding job of taking classic stories and producing some of the best audios out there. Focus also does a great job with Adventures in Odyssey, a continuing story about the people of the town Odyssey (www.whitsend.org). My kids listened to those audios long past the time they would admit it to their teenage friends.

Here are some of my and my friends' favorite chapter books that you can find in an audio version:

The Chronicles of Narnia by C.S. Lewis

Charlie and the Chocolate Factory by Roald Dahl

Hank the Cowdog by John R. Erickson

Charlotte's Web by E.B. White

Magic Tree House by Mary Pope Osborne

Winnie-the-Pooh by A.A. Milne

Cheaper by the Dozen by Frank B. Gilbreth Jr.
    and Ernestine Gilbreth Carey

Treasure Island by Robert Louis Stevenson

The Little Prince by Antoine de Saint-Exupery

Where the Red Fern Grows by Wilson Rawls

The Lord of the Rings by J.R.R. Tolkien

The Adventures of Tom Sawyer by Mark Twain

The Secret Garden by Frances Hodgson Burnett

Redwall by Brian Jacques

Anne of Green Gables by L.M. Montgomery

Ramona the Brave by Beverly Cleary

The Borrowers by Mary Norton

The Cricket in Times Square by George Selden

The Tale of Despereaux by Kate DiCamillo

Pippi Longstocking by Astrid Lindgren

The Wind in the Willows by Kenneth Grahame

Stuart Little by E.B. White

All Creatures Great and Small by James Herriot

Make Connecting Work

I would say that a good 25 percent of the power struggles I had with my kiddos happened in my minivan.

One day Kimber (who is what parenting experts would call a "strong-willed child") was riding in the backseat of my car, snuggly tucked into her car seat. I knew she wouldn't take kindly to the next errand we were running: I was dropping something off to the mother of one of her little friends, but we weren't going inside to play. It was a drive-by drop-off.

Kim was having none of it. She wanted to see her friend and was letting me know in no uncertain terms that this plan was not OK with her.

I pulled out my best parenting. I told her (while she was screaming at the top of her lungs) that she needed to pipe down, sit down, and calm down. I wasn't going to put up with any of her nonsense.

To my surprise, she did what I said. I felt there should have been someone there to hand me some parenting swag. An award? A medal? Something.

I dropped off the package at my friend's house, parking the car in her driveway so I didn't have to get the kids out of the car. I was back in about two minutes, feeling victorious.

That was, until I sat in the driver's seat.

Squish.

I looked in the back of the car, and Justen (who is two years older than Kimberly) just pointed at his sister and said, "She did it."

That little girl had wiggled out of her car seat, jumped into the driver's seat, pulled off her diaper, and whizzed in my seat. She then put her diaper back on and got back into her car seat, all in about two minutes.

This is not what I would call a "connecting time" with my daughter. (And I know some of you parents are thinking to yourselves, *Oh, there would have been a connecting time...on her rear end.*)

I want you to have happier memories in your car.

Teen Challenges

This audiobooks-in-the-car habit has continued as my kids have gone into their young adult years. Although we don't have the school car trips that we once did, we still have the occasional family car trip for vacation, a trip to grandma's house, or when my daughter accompanies me on a work trip.

Here are some suggested titles your teens and young adults might enjoy:

> *Tell Me Where It Hurts* by Nick Trout
>
> *The Help* by Kathryn Stockett
>
> *The No. 1 Ladies' Detective Agency* series
>   by Alexander McCall Smith
>
> *I'm a Stranger Here Myself* and *A Walk in the Woods*
>   by Bill Bryson
>
> *The Prize Winner of Defiance, Ohio* by Terry Ryan
>
> *Skipping Christmas* by John Grisham

Finally, we've also enjoyed *A Prairie Home Companion* by Garrison Keillor. This radio program is family friendly, filled with comedy, and my kids were able to quote the routines for years. Check out http://prairiehome.publicradio.org for broadcast schedules and to find out about downloading archived programs.

Step It Up

Jeremy and I would often have long, silent trips back and forth to his college. Normally I would have plopped in an audiobook, but Jeremy really preferred silence; he was not an audiobook kinda guy.

Then one day when I picked him up, I was listening to a comedy album. When I realized that I had Jer in the car, I went to turn it off. Jeremy, looking straightforward, said, "You can keep listening to it if you want."

So I took my finger off the off button, and Jer and I laughed our way home. After that, it was my mission to find clean, funny comedians for us to listen to in the car together. We would listen to John Pinette and Garrison Keillor, Jim Gaffigan, and Tim Hawkins and laugh and repeat lines.

Suggestions for Singles

Since time and money were always issues when I was single, books on CD (or iPod) were an unguilty pleasure. We would check out CDs at the library and listen to them every time we got in the car. We got hundreds of dollars and hundreds of hours of entertainment for free.

Connecting with Each Personality

Expressive

Capitalize on your expressive child's creative imagination making up a "never-ending story" together. Start with the classic line "Once upon a time, there was a…" and then ask him to describe the first character. Weave his input into a story that continues for a few sentences before you pause to ask for another key detail. This will give him something special to look forward to each time you hop in the car together. (Warning: This can keep going for years. Literally!)

Analytical

Your analytical child is a noticer. She reads billboards, storefront advertising, and street signs. And she analyzes it all. You can sneak a peek into her thinking and gain some deep insights by asking her what she's noticing and what she thinks of it. Develop the habit of listening and asking follow-up questions, and you'll learn a lot about her and her unique way of viewing the world.

Driving

A good debate is a great time passer for you and your driving child. In the neutral territory of your car, with nothing for him to do, you can kill time (but not each other) with a rousing disagreement. Pick a hot topic you can both emotionally detach from (his Saturday night curfew won't work for this) and go at it with gusto. Do stay within the bounds of fair debate rules, especially if there are others in the vehicle with you who might be traumatized by raised voices and name-calling.

Amiable

Turn your van into a duet (or trio or quartet or...) on wheels by singing favorite songs together. Mix it up: sing along with the radio or favorite CDs or raise the roof singing a cappella together. Yes, even if you *hate* your voice. Your amiable child loves you and will love singing *with* you!

Bonus Connections

50 Ways to Connect
with Your Kids

1. Volunteer at a soup kitchen or other local charity in your area.
2. Color pictures together.
3. Do an art or craft project.
4. Take a kickboxing class.
5. Bake cupcakes or cookies and then decorate.
6. Download a free e-book and read it together.
7. Play dress-up.
8. Go on a nature walk.
9. Make homemade play dough.
10. Cook a meal together.
11. Play a sport together (kickball, hoops, softball, soccer).
12. Play Scrabble or another board game.
13. Read stories about heroes and heroines in the Bible.
14. Sing at the top of your lungs to the radio.
15. Make cards for family and friends.
16. Make paper bag puppets.

17. Have a dance party/contest.

18. Write them a note telling them how much you love them and are proud of them.

19. Make a macaroni necklace.

20. Look at photo albums.

21. Go garage sale-ing.

22. Go to a museum.

23. Have a tea party for stuffed animals and/or play figures.

24. Make a book using pictures from magazines.

25. Stack pillows/cushions to make a fort.

26. Plant a garden.

27. Take funny pictures of each other laughing and playing around.

28. Have a picnic.

29. Make your own banana splits with toppings and sprinkles.

30. Download a new iPad app and play together.

31. Go listen to live music.

32. Give a backrub.

33. Write letters to soldiers.

34. Go camping (even if just in the backyard).

35. Make homemade bubbles.

36. Go on a bike ride.

37. Build something with blocks or Legos.

38. Play minigolf.

39. Create an iSpy mission together.

40. Make popcorn and watch movie of their choosing.

41. Go bowling.

42. Play flashlight tag.

43. Go on a scavenger hunt.

44. Learn a magic trick.

45. Start a collection.

46. Make a video of them performing an awesome stunt.

47. Watch funny YouTube videos.

48. Create a secret family code.

49. Make slime with Elmer's glue, borax, and water.

50. Search for insects with a magnifying glass.

Connecting with Your Kids FAQs

Here's a newsflash: Not every family has a white picket fence and 2.4 kids and a fuzzy golden retriever named Molly. And when you're trying to connect with stepkids or manage life as a single mom or survive one of the inevitable "I'd rather connect with Snooki than my mom" phases, things can get a bit sticky (and I'm not talking about the kind of sticky that comes with connecting over a pan of my famous caramel pecan rolls).

I get that. I have a blended family. I get what it's like to coparent and single parent and blended parent and even parent behind a white picket fence. And because of that, I made sure to include tips and suggestions for all types of families in every chapter of this book.

But I still felt like something was missing. And the last thing I wanted to do was leave you with sticky fingers (and no wet wipes) before you started connecting with your kids. So, I asked a few of my smart, savvy friends to help me write this handy FAQs guide full of tips, suggestions, and ideas for parents who want to connect with their kids regardless of their family situation.

FAQs About Connecting with Your Kids When Co-parenting
Answered by Gretchen Schiller

Question: *"I'm divorced, and if I'm being honest, I'm not a huge fan of my ex. I don't want my interactions with my kids to be poisoned by negativity, but that's how I feel most of the time. What can I do?"*

First things first—change the frame. I found this simple technique helped soften my heart tremendously toward my ex-husband. I started viewing my ex solely as my daughter's dad. Granted, this is not always feasible (or realistic) in every interaction. However, I found it helpful for simple day-to-day interactions.

So, when he would come to pick up our daughter, I would greet him as if he were a parent picking up his child after a play date. (Even if you have unfinished business on the table, in front of your child is not the place to discuss it or act visibly irritated.) I would open my front door, greet him with a smile, and welcome him into my home. (Important to note: Whether or not he comes in is completely up to him. If he declines, it does not affect you emotionally any more than any other parent declining.) I would continue giving him a detailed report of how *his* child was during the time she spent at my house.

Here's a trick that seems to work: visualize yourself at your child's school play. Imagine that you see your ex-husband there. Now visualize seeing him as if he were simply one of the other parents in the crowd. Again, this isn't always feasible nor is it always realistic; but I found it helpful in day-to-day interactions.

Question: *"Every time my kids do something with my ex, I sit at home seething, feeling sulky, lonely, and—worst of all—jealous. How do I encourage them to connect with their dad in spite of my feelings?"*

My ex-husband and I divorced two years ago when our daughter was three years old. I'm challenged daily with the choice to bloom in my role as a mother by encouraging the relationship between my daughter and her father or deny them time together, succumbing to the very demons that ruined my marriage. Hmmm…strengthen their father-daughter bond or allow toxic poison from the divorce to seep into her life?

We're moms. Therefore warriors. We fight for the emotional health of our children. Our mantra? The 4Ps: Positive Proactive co-Parenting with a whole lotta Patience.

Every sacrifice softens my heart, and I grow as a mother and ex-wife. My co-parenting relationship with my ex is constantly evolving. I work hard to nurture the relationship between him and our daughter. After all, we are still a family, just two different homes. And frankly, who wants to be angry at someone they have to speak with daily for the rest of their lives?

I've been facedown, sobbing, doubled over in pain trying to co-parent well. It will happen again to me...and to you. We should stay down as long as it takes to heal. Hope is always beside us, ready to move forward when we are. We're fighting to give our children the life they deserve. We grasp hope and start walking—it doesn't matter how slowly—toward restoring grace in our hearts, kindness in our words, and love between our child and our ex-husband.

There were thousands of small decisions I made to screw up my marriage. I am proud when I make one of the thousands of decisions to get the friendship right. Each success is a win for my daughter's future. A win for God.

By the way, that hope we talked about? That's Jesus.

FAQs About Connecting with Your Kids in a Blended Family
Answered by Carol Boley

Question: *"I want to connect with my stepchildren, but honestly, I hardly know them. How do I start connecting when we don't have a shared history yet?"*

First, make every effort to deliberately show love to your stepchildren without expecting a response from them. Do it because it's the right thing to do. Do it because you love Jesus. Do it whether or not you have the feelings to go with it. Feelings are not the key. Then, accept that it is normal for stepchildren to reject you. Don't take rejection personally. Often it is directed toward your role as *the stepmother*, not the wonderful person you really are. Likewise, accept that it is normal for you not to feel the same intensity of love for a stepchild that you do for a natural child. No guilt here!

It's absolutely essential for you to accept your stepchildren just as they are—regardless of the emotional baggage they carry with them and their feelings toward you. You have had no chance to influence anything about them before they became your stepchildren. They are who they are. Disregard any temptation to judge or condemn them. Acceptance of them goes a long way toward connection with them. Give it time. It takes three to five years for a stepfamily to begin to emerge. Don't quit. Don't give up. You are in this for the long haul. The best thing you can do for your stepchildren is provide a stable family. Be patient as everyone gets used to each other. Don't destroy a path to connection over a relatively minor issue.

Lastly, make it your goal to compliment each child daily. Even if a pleasing color choice in clothing is the best you can do, let them know you find them capable and competent, maybe even brilliant. Also, notice every positive thing your stepchildren do or say, no matter how small. Celebrate. There are no small victories. Be sure to brag on them both in private and in front of their dad.

Question: *"How do I connect with my stepchildren when I see them only every other weekend?"*

When stepchildren visit, give them at least a thirty-minute transition time to adjust from another house and its set of rules to your house and your set of rules. Make sure you and your husband have agreed on the rules for all the children in your home and the consequences for breaking them. Then be sure to follow through. This helps to establish trust and security, as well as encourage good behavior.

Then, make your visits with them fun! Capitalize on any common interests. You probably will seem more intelligent and fascinating to your stepkids if you share some of their interests. Nothing in common?

Enter their world by allowing them to teach you a new skill or hobby, or at least tell you about theirs. Even let them invite their friends over to your home for game night, dinner, or if your budget allows, to go with you on a special outing.

Take note of favorite foods and serve them often, whether meals or snacks. Be aware of and honor any special dietary needs or choices (sugar-free, gluten-free, vegetarian) even if it means more work for you. Rent their favorite movies, or let them choose an appropriate movie when the entire family goes out. Even give your stepchildren the gift of time alone with their dad. Then take advantage of the time to get a manicure or spend some much-needed girlfriend time.

Also, not having full-time custody doesn't mean you can't make them an important part of your life. For each stepchild, keep a special place in your home that belongs to them alone. If they don't have their own room (and that's OK; no need for guilt if they don't), how about their own drawer? Or closet?

Then, even when it's not your official time with them, make every effort to show up at their sporting events, plays, and concerts. Show them they are a priority to you—you care about them and you value them even when you're not with them.

Question: *"My stepdaughter is not my biggest fan. She looks at me as the outsider who encroached upon her happy little family. How do I build a relationship with her when she's made it clear that she doesn't like me?"*

My first piece of advice is to always model the behavior you want them to copy. Because they will. Eventually. Or they will at least notice. Even things like saying please and thank you and smiling at them. Don't nag, complain, or whine. Speak kind words in a kind tone of voice. No ridiculing or cutting comments. Even if sarcasm is normal for your stepfamily, it's best if you don't use it until everyone is comfortable with each other and accepted by each other. At least initially, as the outsider, you are not allowed. Bite your tongue if you must. Better a bloody tongue than a wounded stepchild. "The tongue has the power of life and death" (Proverbs 18:21).

Eight of the most powerful words you can use are: "I'm sorry. I was wrong. Please forgive me." Likewise, forgive them quickly for every offense. Why not? If you don't, you will be consumed by bitterness, anger, frustration, possibly even hatred, and can wind up making yourself physically sick. "Be kind and compassionate to one another, forgiving each other, just as in Christ God forgave you" (Ephesians 4:32). Think something they say or do is too tough to forgive? Ask Jesus to forgive them through you. Nothing is too difficult for him, and it will strengthen your relationship with him as you experience his work in you.

Don't get drawn into an argument. Do not "take the bait." Practice reflective listening. Listen for the feelings behind the words. "It sounds like you're feeling discouraged. How can I help?" If they are angry with you, keep using reflective listening and don't get defensive. "The words of the reckless pierce like swords, but the tongue of the wise brings healing" (Proverbs 12:18).

Pray for them. Choose specific and encouraging verses to pray over them, out loud if they are receptive, or just between God and you. Don't use verses to beat them up or condemn them, even if your motivation is to offer guidance. Stick to a blessing. "Do not let your hearts be troubled" (John 14:1) is a good start. Treat and talk to all children in your family with equal respect. Be aware of any tendencies to show favoritism. While stepchildren may try to throw that accusation in your face, make sure it is just that…an accusation and not truth.

Finally, never criticize them, their friends, their father, or their bio-mom, even if she is serving time in the state pen as an ax murderer. There very well may be character flaws in all these people, but it is not your job to point them out. To your stepchildren, criticism of these people sounds a lot like criticism of them. And it makes a stepmother look small.

When disappointed in stepchildren's behavior, be sure to differentiate them from their actions. What they do is different than who they are.

FAQs About Connecting with Your Kids When Your Kids Don't Want to Connect

Answered by Ellen Schuknecht (FamilyWings.org)

Question: *"We're going through a bit of a rough patch at our house, and my son seems to think he'd be better off not having parents at all. How do I connect with him when there is so much tension between us?"*

When my oldest was in middle school, she decided that I was without a doubt the stupidest, most annoying, and most utterly humiliating person who had ever lived. Naturally, that didn't lead to many opportunities to connect with her. But I had to remind myself that as the adult in the relationship, it was my responsibility to take the high road.

So regardless of her attitude and her actions, I always made sure to be available to her. I made her breakfast and hung out in the kitchen while she ate, happily chattering about anything and everything, hoping she'd interject. I sent little notes to her in her lunchbox. I asked her for her opinion. Most of all, I made sure that she knew that I loved her regardless of the state of our relationship.

This doesn't mean letting a misbehaving kid get by with murder. You can establish rules, deliver consequences, and provide discipline while also being an encourager and working to connect with your kids. For example, when my daughter was in her mom-knows-nothing phase, we had a rule that if she wanted to rant, rave, and be disrespectful, she could do it behind the closed door to her room. But if she was with us in the rest of the house, we expected respect. We enforced that rule, always, but whenever she did come out of her room and spend time with us, we made sure that our time together was encouraging—and resisted the impulse to nag, yell, or be disrespectful toward her.

Question: *"With two outgoing siblings, my shy daughter seems to get lost in the shuffle. How do I make sure she gets the time, encouragement, and connection that she needs?"*

When my kids were little, I noticed a pattern: Whenever my son started getting low grades in school, acting out at home, or leaving his

room messy, it usually meant that he needed our one-on-one attention. His natural reaction was to fade backward—while my two gre-
garious daughters grabbed the attention they needed. My introverted
middle child simply didn't know how to ask for what he needed and
didn't have a personality that demanded it.

So I made the habit of escaping with my son for one-on-one time—
whether it was taking him out for dinner or going bowling together—
to give him a chance to just talk. And lo and behold, every time I got
him away from his chatterbox sisters, he would open up and share with
me whatever was going on.

My advice is to work hard to recognize the different personality
types of your kids and come up with strategies to connect with them
and their unique needs. For my son, that meant one-on-one time away
from his sisters. For other kids, it may mean family time. Or project
time. Or time outdoors. Whatever it is, make sure your kids get the
time to connect with you in the way that they best connect.

Dear Reader,

Thanks for being a part of *The Mom Project*. One of the greatest privileges I have is to hear back from the people who have used my books. I would love to stay in touch.

Email: **info@KathiLipp.com**

Facebook: **facebook.com/kathilipp.author**

Twitter: **twitter.com/kathilipp**

Mail: Kathi Lipp
171 Branham Lane
Suite 10-122
San Jose, CA 95136

Opportunities for input and discussion with other readers are available at **www.KathiLipp.com**.

In His Grace,

Kathi Lipp

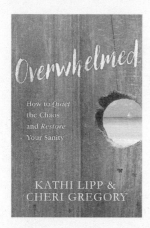

Overwhelmed

Kathi Lipp and Cheri Gregory

Feeling overwhelmed? Wondering if it's possible to move from "out of my mind" to "in control" when you've got too many projects on your plate and too much mess in your relationships?

Kathi and Cheri want to show you five surprising reasons why you become stressed, why social media solutions don't often work, and how you can finally create a plan that works for you. As you identify your underlying hurts, uncover hope, and embrace practical healing, you'll become equipped to...

- trade the to-do list that controls you for a calendar that allows space in your life
- decide whose feedback to forget and whose input to invite
- replace fear of the future with peace in the present

You *can* simplify and savor your life—guilt free! Clutter, tasks, and relationships may overwhelm you now, but God can help you overcome with grace.